RATTLED AWAKE: VOLUME TEN

The Liberty Issue

Rattled Awake Authors

Lonnee Rey

CONTENTS

NICOLE ANGAI-GALINDO...
DYING TO LIVE

The ambiance while sitting here in my living room, about to write my chapter, is perfect. Fitting for the story to follow; another of my Rattled Awake moments. In another hour or so, the moon will be up. The blinds are drawn now, earlier than usual. The shadows, being cast in the room from the one inch slits of light, coming through the vertical gaps in the blinds, loom behind me. I feel their eyes staring holes into the back of my neck. They are troubled by what I am about to share, for when I bring them into the light, they no longer exist.

I had to find a way to survive this again or lose everyone I loved, and all the ground I had covered since the last time I fell to my knees. If I didn't, I feared that all the other times that I'd been here, one step closer to my death, would now be one time too many. Death was what awaited me, if I didn't find a way.

◆ ◆ ◆

The soreness in the fleshy part of my palms lingered days after the incident, even though the redness had since disappeared. Staring at the ceiling fan whirling slowly above me, that horrific morning drive to work a week ago, played through slowly in my mind..even slower than the sluggish movement of the ceiling fan.

A red light and the screeching of tires beside me shook me out of my daze. It did so thankfully, so that I could slam my foot on the brake. I wondered as I glanced to my left, was the woman at the wheel in the car beside me watching her life crumble before her eyes as well? Did she feel it? Feel it coming? What was she going to do about it? I shivered. Was she really there or was the little voice being sucked down into the quicksand that was my logic, throwing out these questions to me?

When the light turned green, I pulled hurriedly over into the next street on my right. I stopped just shy of the edge of the driveway belonging to the last house on the cul de sac. Suddenly, my arms flew up into the air, grazing the cool vinyl ceiling of my truck. Just as suddenly, my arms crashed down. My palms hit the steering wheel so hard that I could feel the vibration up to my elbows. In a rhythmic movement, I kept repeating the rise and fall of my arms. Each time that my open palms hit the steering wheel I screamed, "Why me? Why Now? I can't do this again!"

I made it to work that day, ten minutes late and with a third berating taken to my desk. I set it beside my other lateness souvenirs...

◆ ◆ ◆

Dragging myself into a sitting position, I gingerly turned left and dropped my feet off the side of the bed. I needed to go to the bathroom. I needed to put the ceiling fan on a higher speed because I could feel the droplets of sweat running down the side of my left temple. I was making my way unsteadily to the corridor that led to the bathroom when I started retching. The disgusting tasting bile filled my mouth. Not wanting to spit it out and make another mess for my husband to clean up when he returned from work, I found the strength to dash to the bathroom.

Back to bed a few minutes later and again the floodgates broke open. This was my third mini-breakdown today. "Could a person really have multiple breakdowns in the span of just one day?" I thought to myself. The first one happened at 6:15AM as my husband was leaving for work. I didn't want him to go because I did not want to be alone. Yet, whenever he was at home, he was sitting perched on the edge of the bed at my side, simply holding my hands in his warm ones, staring intently at me while I said nothing.

My tummy was growling. I couldn't remember when was the last time that I ate something.

I could smell the spiciness of the roasting jalapenos in the air, my eyes slightly burning. I loved working in my in-laws Mexican restaurant with my husband. We were in the throes of covid and I knew so many people were trapped in their homes. I felt lucky to be able to have somewhere to go every day. We served takeout, over a table set up at the front door.

How funny that I was working in a Spanish restaurant. Me, a Trinidadian-born woman, trying to recall the five years of this foreign language that I'd mastered enough to get an outstanding grade upon high school graduation.

Months later, when I did return to my full-time office job, I would still work at the restaurant part-time. Well, it was full-time hours around a part-time schedule. Between the two jobs I was putting in four sixteen hour days a week and two twelve hour days on the weekend. I was happily exhausted until that exhaustion caught up to me, forcing me on a downward spiral.

It was a slow spiral that began with me trying to hold on, digging my fingernails into the surface of reality.

I lost the battle.

On my way down, I caught glimpses of the empty antidepressant bottles rolling around at the back of the top drawer in the bathroom vanity. I heard the clinking of the empty beer bottles stuffed into doubled thirteen gallon drawstring plastic bags, as I snuck out the front door to take them to the garbage cans at the side of the house.

Friday's five and Saturday's six plus the doubles on a weeknight after reaching home at 11PM. I had been drinking about a case of beer a week.

Legs swung off the side of the bed for the second time today, I dragged my feet going into the kitchen. I opened the refrigerator. Of course there was no beer in it. When I crashed, my husband popped the cap off of each bottle of beer that was left in the refrigerator and poured the bitter, golden liquid down the drain.

To this day I still crave that first icy sip from the salt rimmed bottle on a scorching Summer day.
It is Summer now and I know that one of these upcoming weekends, I will have to fight back the urge. Yet after the second sip, I'm so turned off.

I reached into the refrigerator and removed a vanilla flavored yogurt. It seemed that I could only get down non-solids these days. Smoothies, jello and soup made up my diet for the last three weeks. "Tomorrow is Saturday." I thought "Or is it?" I'd lost track of which day of the week it was. If so, then our telehealth call was at 9AM. 'Our' telehealth call because my husband participated in these each week, wanting to hear what my psychiatrist had to say about the progress he reported.

I certainly didn't feel as if any progress were being made. Have you ever felt that no matter how hard you are trying, you aren't getting anywhere? I felt as if I were swimming with all my upper body strength, against the strongest current which was only keeping me in the same spot.

◆ ◆ ◆

That evening, after my husband returned from work, he got me out of my robe and into a tee and jogging pants. He had to double knot the drawstring after cinching in the waistband because the pants were sliding off my skinny hips. He half dragged, half carried me to the back porch and gently eased me into our rocking chair. The one that he had in the bedroom of his apartment when we were dating. The one I would rock back and forth in while imitating rowing a boat and singing row, row, row your boat. Then we would look at each other and both burst out laughing.

Where had that woman gone? It seemed that every now and then over the last forty four years of my life I would lose her.

As the third week rolled into the forth, I slowly started gaining my strength back. The combination of medication that I had been prescribed was working its way back into my system. Two antidepressants, Celexa and Wellbutrin, plus a mood stabilizer, Lamotragine. My appetite slowly started returning and I could keep down some solids. Every day my sister would call on her lunch break to see how I was doing. We would chat for ten or fifteen minutes and then I would go back and lay down.

An hour or so later, I would get back up and sit at the

couch which faced the sliding doors that opened onto the back porch. Just a week ago, I would not draw the blinds. Now I did. I sat at a folding dinner table, building a puzzle from the dollar store. This became my weekday routine. By the time my two month short-term disability came to an end, I had pieced together three five-hundred piece puzzles and completed a fifteen hundred piece one that I had started a month before I fell apart. It seemed that building puzzles was the only thing that distracted me from the emptiness in my brain, the numbness in my heart. Even so, a turmoil of emotions crawled along the surface of my skin incessantly.

One morning, a few weeks later I gathered up our dirty laundry into the three plastic color coordinated baskets, loaded them into our pickup, and sent my husband a text message that I was going to the laundromat. He immediately dialed back and when I answered, I knew he knew that I was going to be ok.

Those were the longest two months of our lives. I had lived the nightmare before, with others, who would not be able to withstand the bipolar blow that I was dealt every time I misstepped or for whatever reason, the universe seemed bored and needed to get a hoot out of messing with my head.

Do you know what it feels like to go from feeling so afraid and helpless that you would not take a shower unless your husband were sitting on the closed toilet seat waiting for you, to get back behind the wheel after two months of not driving? You may never have lived this exact scenario but I bet that every single one of you have felt both powerless at times and then empowered again.

The sad truth is that I had seen it coming. It was not my first ferris wheel ride. I knew that with the controls unmanned every top of ride would not result with a seamless 180 to the bottom of ride. I knew that unmanned it would feel like the most twisted, fearsome, heart-plunging roller coaster ever built... and I hated rides. Knowing that never stopped me from jumping on the damn ride before, but this time was the worst. A few days on the ride was one thing. Eight weeks, a whole other story.

Two months before I went out on STD, my husband had lost his job due to Covid. He started a new job two weeks after I had to step away from mine. We cleaned-out our modest savings, and the disability check, a whopping $171 a week, just about covered the psychiatrist fee without medical benefits. The $50 left over each week went toward my medication.

A combination of working myself almost to death, self medicating with alcohol, and being irresponsible about managing my bipolar medicine, almost cost me my life. Again. Though drinking had not been a part of the mix before, overworking myself was nothing new to me.

Strangely, I haven't completed a puzzle since. I have saved them all however. My husband carefully taped them all at the back and one of them sits on my desk at work now. The big one. The fifteen hundred piece one. A reminder yes, of a period in my life where ill-made and oftentimes ill-fitting puzzle pieces, purchased for a buck for 500 saved my life. It kept my hands moving and my mind thinking while the medication my brain needed did its thing.

"Life is like a box of chocolates." - Forrest Gump.

Or, is it like a puzzle?

"Life is like a puzzle." - Nic, the Gifted Bipolar Writer

Each piece is not meant to be placed until it's time. You will spot the pieces and it may convey something to you, though you don't know what just yet. Perhaps it's a bit of color that will catch your eye, the curve of an outline, the shadow on a piece of white but until that piece is meant to be placed, it will not fit. The picture will not become clear until all of the pieces are placed. I held onto building those puzzles during that time. I know now it was as a way to maintain control; control over something when everything else around me, or rather, within me, was spinning out of control.

Once I took back control of my life (with the help of medication and talk-therapy), the universe knew better than to mess with me.

That last fall, the one I had to forgive myself for so that I could heal, was in 2020. On July 1st of 2021 we purchased our first home. A year later, my husband, who was brought to the USA by his parents when he was five years old, and who had lived here his whole life trying to attain legal status, got his green card. Later this year, he will be eligible to apply for his American citizenship.

The job that I returned to after my two month absence, the one where on the first day of my return I was sat down in the conference room and told by the vice president, to never discuss what happened with any of my co-workers, is now history. I'd been to hell and back and I'd be damned if the person that signed my paycheck felt that he owned my life enough, so that he could tell me what I could and could not share with others.

I've spent the last few years living a life of gratitude. Finding joy in the simple things, like savoring a good cup of coffee while sitting on the back stoop, looking onto our beautiful backyard. It's surrounded by trees on the perimeter but flat for the two hundred feet it extends to the wooded area at the back, where the deer like to wander in from and nibble at whatever it is they seem to feast on.

The day after this book launch, July 5th, will be the second year anniversary with my company. I walked into this one wearing my bipolarness on my sleeve. Like my boss says, "Nicole is a storm system, you have to see what's coming before it hits." They know who I am, where my heart is; they give me the space and the grace I need when I need it. As a result, my focus and my work are one hundred times what it's ever been.

I will never again hide who I am from anyone. I will never again ignore the whispered voice that I know belongs to me and the almost imperceptible message it carries. Imperceptible because of all the noise of the world around me drowning it out.

You must stay in tune to the pitch of that whisper. You must trust it to guide you and stop and heed what it's telling you. Your very life depends on it. Mine did and because I didn't heed it, I almost lost it.

We all have the survival instinct within us but that does not guarantee that we will all survive. In fact, some will never again step into the light because they have lived in the dark for too long. Sharing my story has helped many people to understand that we must first embrace that which we think is so wrong with us, as the very thing that can be so right about us. It is the thing that pushes us to take the broken pieces and make ourselves whole again.

And, once you are whole again, you will want nothing more than to help others bring their shadows into the light, so they no longer exist.

Nicole Angai-Galindo, aka Nic, is on a mission to show the world that having a mental illness does not determine the level of happiness and success that one can achieve in life. She is known to many on her social media platform of choice, LinkedIn, as *The Gifted Bipolar Writer.* She co-authored three International Best-Selling anthologies in 2023, including Rattled Awake Vol. 1 - the Flagship book.

At the end of 2023, she published her first anthology, *A Note To My Family– I Am Your Legacy.* Nic is in the process of publishing her second anthology, *A LinkedIn Love Affair.* She is also the host (ess) of N.I.C. Never In Control the Live Show, the spinoff of her live audio room. When she is not running her part-time business, The Gifted Bipolar Writer, Nic, works full-time in the elevator industry.

She jokes that she is made in the U.S. with Trinidadian parts!

https://www.linkedin.com/in/nicthegbw/

https://www.amazon.com/Note-My-Family-Your-Legacy/dp/B0CPQ3NVJR

Nic at her desk in work with the 1500 piece puzzle she talks about in her story. The ornamental plaque on her desk behind the puzzle, is a souvenir she picked up a year after her short-term disability, during a trip to Canada to visit her sister.

It reads, "She believed she could, so she did."

REFLECTIONS FROM NIC & RICK

As soon as I heard the title, "Rattled Awake," I knew I had to contribute my story to this anthology. It was an earth-shattering experience for me writing in the flagship book, Volume One.

It was an incredible opportunity to learn so much and write alongside stellar co-authors. I am humbled and honored to be a returning author in Volume 10 and look forward to a familiar yet new experience!

Rick Incorvia
Rattled Awake: The Writers & Poets Edition

"Rattled Awake: The Writers & Poets Edition," was a great experience for this weary, and aging, author. Collaborating with young, passionate writers of so many different styles invigorated my imagination. Lonnee Rey is a breath of fresh air and manages the workshop like a true pro. AuthorRickIncorvia.com & Facebook

REFLECTIONS FROM LISA

Lisa Marree
Rattled Awake: Volumes Three & Five

It only takes one person with a vision to create an impactful movement, and the Rattled Awake Anthology Series is doing just that, as Volume 10 is here, on the jet stream of 9 Volumes in 9 months ALL #1 Best Sellers. Incredible! The creator, publisher and Editor in Chief, the very talented, caring, purpose driven Lonnee Rey, who has given voice and opened doors to over 60 co-authors so far.

I am honored to have written a chapter in Volumes 3 and 5, sharing how I have turned tragedy and pain into power, that has not only impacted me personally and professionally, but has impacted readers and opened business doors. I encourage you to share your story and start here in the Rattled Awake Anthology 'movement', it may just change your life! Website

JASON WILSON...INSIDE THE DREAM WORLD

Morpheus: Have you ever had a dream, Neo, that you were so sure was real? (The Matrix: 1999)

Did you know that the dream world or spirit world is just as real as the physical world in which you live? If you ever had any doubts, I'm here to tell you, IT IS!

In a lucid dream, how is it that you have your sense of sight, hearing, touch and smell just as if you were awake? The short answer to this is that you are an ETERNAL SPIRIT created by God, not just a physical body.

There are three parts to a man or woman: the spirit, body and soul. Your spirit and soul actually leave your physical body every night and travel into the dream world or spiritual dimension. Your soul is the same as the mind, which allows you to think, choose and sense things in the spiritual dimension. God uses dreams to give us revelatory knowledge of things that are important to us.

There are twenty categories of spiritual dreams. The following account is a WARNING DREAM, in which God tells you to do or not do something. For example: Don't go home a certain way.

In October of 2011, I hadn't had a conversation with my

mother back in Atlanta for about two months, which was unusual. God placed her in my spirit to give her a call. When she answered the phone, I knew right away by the tone of her distraught voice that something was off.

I asked her how she was doing and she said, "Not so good." Our conversation only lasted for about 10 minutes. I knew that she wasn't able to give me any real information because her boyfriend was in the room. She spoke to me with only one- or two-word answers and it gave me the unsettling feeling that something was really wrong. Her boyfriend, who I couldn't stand and who no one else in the family liked, was a warlock who practiced black magic and had a narcissistic personality. He exhibited an uncanny control over her that gravely affected her physical and mental health.

She met him after she and my father separated after being married for 25 years. At the beginning of their relationship, he made a good impression and seemed really courteous and friendly. However, as time passed, her behavior became more and more erratic. The decisions she was making with her finances were completely out of the ordinary, and would periodically spend an exorbitant amount of money on stuff that she didn't need. She started drinking alcohol, smoking marijuana and developed insomnia. Her personality completely changed to the point that no one recognized her. Some time later, she was diagnosed with Bi-polar depression and made her first suicide attempt.

One day, while driving to work, she made the decision to pull over to the side of the expressway in downtown

Atlanta, smoke a cigarette, get out of her car and proceed to walk across into on-coming traffic. A truck driver came to a screeching halt, traffic was stopped and the paramedics took her to the hospital. Those were the beginnings of my mother's mental health decline.

Her boyfriend would do things like take her to the ATM on the day that she received her retirement check, and have her withdraw all the money to spend it on whatever he wanted. As a result, her rent, car note and other bills weren't being paid.

I hung up the phone and that night during my prayer time, I told God that something was terribly wrong with my mother back home. I asked him to show me in a dream what was happening. I went to sleep and had a lucid dream.

I was at the top of a tall building in a city downtown and I saw a huge bus full of people about to fall off the edge. Inside the bus, people were panicking as the bus filled up with turquoise-blue colored water. All I could do was stand there in shock and amazement as I wondered where the water came from.

The bus fell off of the edge of the building and crashed to the ground. I went down to the street, opened the door to the bus and all the turquoise-blue water gushed out. I entered the bus to find that everybody was dead, but my mother was among them at the back of the bus and alive. I pulled her out and then I woke up.

I said, "Dear God, I have no idea what's going on in

Atlanta, but I need to get on a flight immediately and get home!" I flew home about a week later and when I got to the airport, red flag #1 was that my mother's boyfriend picked me up at the airport in her car. Red flag #2 was upon seeing my mother. Of course I was happy to see her, but I was also in a state of shock as my mouth hung open. She had lost a lot of weight and had no hair on the top of her head! I knew that to lose her hair like that she had to have been under a great amount of undue stress from dealing with her boyfriend and lack of finances.

After a few days, I noticed that she spent the majority of her time in the bed and didn't want to leave the house. Her favorite shows to watch on TV had to do with murder and criminal investigation. One of them, a show called "Snapped," is about how people had gotten to a breaking point and killed their cheating loved ones. One episode was about how a woman who found out her husband had cheated on her. To kill him, she mixed Coke and antifreeze in a cup and gave it to her husband. He drank it, got sick and went to the emergency room. Twenty-four hours later, he was dead.

My mother kept a Quick Trip styrofoam cup on her night stand with a straw and a lid on it. I paid no real attention to it until one day, she brought it up in conversation.

She said, "Do you see this cup here on my nightstand?" I said, "Yeah."
"Take a look inside."
I took the lid off and asked her, "What is this???"
"Well, it's a mix of soda and antifreeze. I was going to drink it and kill myself. If you hadn't gotten on a plane

and come here when you did, I would be dead right now."

Do you want to know the color of the liquid inside the cup on my mother's night stand?

It was turquoise-blue, the same color of the water that was inside the bus in my dream!

To say the least, I was completely flabbergasted at my mother's words and the reality of what she was saying began to sink in.

It finally hit me. Oh my God, taking action after having a dream saved my mother from killing herself!

Having this supernatural experience gave me the urgency of wanting to find out more about what God was telling me in my dreams. I didn't know at the time what all the symbols from my dream meant or even how to interpret the context of it. I just knew that I had to get home as soon as I could.

Later, I studied dream interpretation from pastors and did research on what dream symbols meant. I became certified as a Life Coach, talked to all of my clients about their supernatural experiences in dreams and started a podcast to interview people on all things supernatural. From those experiences talking to executives, entrepreneurs, athletes, entertainers, psychics, demonologists and UFO investigators, I decided to become a Spiritual Dream Coach. From there, I was able to interpret the dream I had with my mother.

The turquoise-blue color of the water is symbolic of revelation and prophecy. The bus is symbolic of the size of the ministry or number of people that would be helped as a result of me walking in my purpose.

God used the dream to tell me in 2011 that the people inside of the bus were suicide victims, but that I would be used by God to prevent my mother's suicide attempt and other people's attempts in the future. I look at my life now and it's all come true.

I thank God for waking up from the dream, heeding the warning of my mom and taking immediate action to go home. Because of God's love, mercy and grace, that trip back home to Atlanta allowed me to spend nine months with my mother. It was the last time that I saw her alive. In 2014, she died of natural causes.

When you have a dream and you're aware that you're dreaming, the first thing that you want to do is to write down everything you remember from what you saw and heard in the dream. Also, take note of how you feel in the dream and when you wake up from it. Do you feel excited, encouraged, inspired, or joyful? Or do you feel fearful, angry, frustrated or sad. That will help to determine the context of the dream.

Include all the symbols you can remember: the people, animals, insects, the weather, time of day, clothing you're wearing, any colors, numbers, mode of transportation and buildings. If you're inside of a house, pay attention to the room you're located in. A house in a dream is symbolic of a mindset or way of thinking. Every room of the house has a particular symbolic meaning. For example, if you're in the kitchen, it's a place where things are being prepared to be eaten and digested. Being located there tells you that there's a life situation God wants you to be prepared for so that you receive the blessings he has for you.

Through dreams, God can let you know what your purpose is, bring you healing, give you a warning to do or not do something, let you know that your character needs to be improved in a particular area, give you ideas, concepts and witty inventions, let you know the plans that darkness has for you and deliver you from evil spirits.

"It shall come about after this That I shall pour out My Spirit on all mankind; And your sons and your daughters will prophesy, Your old men will dream dreams, Your young men will see visions." (Joel 2:28) AMP

Today, I'm the CEO of Circle Of Friends Club, a mental wellness community and resource. My mental wellness podcast show is called Circle Back To You.

I Define A Mental Health Issue As

A Spiritual Battle That Takes Place In The Mind.

The reason why you may not remember your dreams is because dark spirits don't want you to know that you're being influenced to be depressed, anxious or suicidal in the spiritual dimension.

Being attacked by a demonic spirit in a dream can affect your body in the physical dimension. Illness, disease, bruising and other examples of physical harm can manifest as a result of what you've experienced.

These spirits have names. A succubus spirit, which attacks men, or an incubus spirit that attacks women, can rape or physically assault you in a dream. The Pavor Nocturnus spirit (night terror) causes you to be paralyzed where you can't move, talk or scream for help. It chokes you and is responsible for SIDS- sudden infant death syndrome. Doctors have coined this phenomenon as "Sleep Paralysis."

The good news is that you can fight these demonic spirits in your dreams by commanding them to leave in the name of Jesus.

As a Spiritual Dream Coach, I take a look at the context of the dream and all the symbols. With the guidance of the Holy Spirit, I can give an interpretation of what God is revealing in the spiritual dimension about your life.

Are you the person who's afraid to share a dream out of thinking that you'll be judged? Are you taking medication for your mental health, going to visits at the psychiatrist and nothing has cured you?

You don't have to suffer in silence. You're not at fault for the self-condemning and suicidal thoughts that you're having. You're being conditioned and influenced to have those thoughts by demonic spirits in the spirit world. I'm the one who will listen to you. There's a reason why you're having these dreams and dream interpretation websites you find on Google aren't the place to go for a spiritual dream interpretation. You can't fight a spiritual battle with anything physical, but there's a way out!

I can help you to get free of being tormented in your thought life.

Contact me today for 2 free Spiritual Dream coaching sessions!

jason@circleoffriendsclub.com
https://www.linkedin.com/in/jwthehealer
https://circleoffriendsclub.com

Jason Wilson, Spiritual Dream Coach and CEO of Circle Of Friends Club, is on a mission to empower people all over the world to use their God given power and authority to overcome depression, anxiety, PTSD and suicidal ideation. His coaching series, "Connection To The Promise" is a guide to successfully navigating the dream world or spiritual dimension in order to
receive healing from trauma, past hurt, unforgiveness and rejection.

Jason's Circle Of Friends Club is a global mental wellness community and resource where
people can make friends, attend events and find the right therapists and coaches. His podcast, "Circle Back To You," features the mental wellness practitioners, entrepreneurs, athletes and entertainers we have featured in the Circle Of Friends Club community.

You can find Jason on Linkedin and his website:

CircleOfFriendsClub.com

REFLECTIONS FROM CHIYEDZA

**Chiyedza Nyahuye
Rattled Awake Volumes 2 & 3**

Being a co-author of Rattled Awake 2 & 3 was a surprising delight in co-creating an instant supportive, safe community, and sharing our vulnerable, heartfelt stories that became International Best Sellers. This led to more opportunities for collaboration, finding myself continuously invited to speak and share in various podcasts and LinkedIn live sessions.

Currently being published in another anthology, Lessons We Learnt From Covid19, which includes a year of developing and implementing business-building strategies with global co-authors. Grateful for this opportunity to see and be seen, rippling exquisite joy, healing, intuitive insights, and inspiration around the world! LinkedIn

ANDREA HORVATH...THE SOULFUL SHIFT

What if you knew you couldn't fail?

That was the conviction I held close to my heart in September 2021.

I was sitting at my desk in my home office and I opened up a new company-wide message from Human Resources.

I felt my heart immediately sink into my stomach.

The moment I saw the subject line of the memo, I knew I was going to lose my job.

Have you ever had those moments where in an instant you know your life is forever changed?

The company I was working for was mandating Covid vaccination to remain employed. I was not vaccinated at the time and did not have any intention of getting them.

My reasons for not getting them are deeply personal and date back to 2004, but that is not what this story is about. Nor is it about whether any of us should or shouldn't have gotten one. In fact, this story isn't about vaccines at all.

I was 49 years old at the time, a single parent of 2 teenage girls. I had 100% custody of my daughters and a mortgage to pay. I had worked for the organization for 11 years and was making six-figures in management as a CPA (Certified Professional Accountant.)

The memo clearly stated that if you did not provide proof of vaccination, it would be in direct conflict with company policy, therefore, you would be fired with cause. This meant zero severance.

I sat there unable to move.

I knew there were companies mandating vaccines, however, I worked from home 100% of the time and the nearest company office was a three-and-a-half-hour drive from my home. I had no physical contact with any people as a part of my job.

There was nothing about this mandate that made sense with my situation.

I have learned in life that if something doesn't make sense, either there is information I don't have, or the person or situation is not in alignment with me. Sometimes it's a combination of both. Overall, it is a sign: time for me to take a step back and strategically determine my next steps.

I emailed Human Resources to double check that I would still need it if I worked from home 100% of the time. The director of HR confirmed.

Deep breath.

Now I had all the facts. The company was clearly not in alignment with my values in a significant way. Not for a single moment did I need to think about what to do.

It didn't even feel like I made a decision. It felt like I followed my soul. It was my truth. I wasn't here to convince anyone to do, or not do, anything. I simply knew that I had to listen to what felt right for me.

It was really only a matter of time and I would be terminated. Eleven years, poof, over in a heartbeat.

I knew that if I were to give into the pressure, it would have meant I didn't trust myself. It would have meant I didn't believe in myself. It would have meant that money meant more to me than honoring myself. It would have meant that their opinion mattered more than mine. It would have meant that I didn't matter.

I may not have mattered to them. What I cared about most in that moment was that I mattered to myself. I cared about the example I was setting for my daughters. I am raising strong, self-assured daughters and I know they are always watching me as an example.

What felt right was to allow myself to be fired.

I'm not going to sugar coat it: the next two weeks were fucking horrendous. On October 14th, in a 90-second Teams call from the Director of Regional Operations, I was let go. No severance. I said nothing. I couldn't get off that call fast enough.

If you have been ever fired or let go from a job, you know that it comes with a mix of emotions. Surprisingly, a huge wave of relief washed over my body like a tidal wave. Not shame, not embarrassment. Relief.

I was totally miserable being an accountant. I had picked it as a career for reasons that were no longer valid. I did what I thought I was supposed to do. I picked it because I was brilliant at math and there would always be jobs available. I didn't believe I had other options.

I had lived the first 33 years of my life as a completely different person than I am now.

I used to be the good girl who followed all the rules. I was the poster child for being a people pleaser. I had always done what was expected of me. I had always followed the "shoulds" in life. Becoming a CPA was part of me following what was expected of me.

When I was 33, life created a perfect storm to shake me out of my slumber. That is a story for another time. However, it was as if life had turned on a light switch, (although it felt more like a gut punch.) And so began the process of ditching the expected path and listening to my own inner voice.

I had my own "Eat, Pray, Love" experience without the exotic world travel. Liz Gilbert truly is my soul sister.

I left my marriage and distanced myself from my family

as I began to forge my own path. I overhauled my personal life, and eventually began to look at my career. I knew an accountant wasn't IT. I knew I was meant for more. Ever since I was a small child I questioned the world.

I remember as a child watching my Mom go to work each day. She would get up early in the morning and put on a suit, which seemed so weirdly bizarre to me as she is a super casual person. She spent so much money on those suits which I didn't understand because we didn't have much money and she was an executive secretary. She would go to work all day, come home exhausted, and start all over the next day. I felt deep down there must be something I'm missing. Why was this just what was accepted?

In more recent years I marveled at how people left their loved ones each day to go do something that totally stressed them out, only to hope to squeeze in a few precious moments of joy on the weekends. This cycle continues for decades taking the best days, months and years of peoples' lives, hoping one day they can retire. As far as I could see this is just being "re" "tired" over and over again. Nothing made sense to me. I questioned it. However, whenever I brought it up to other people, they looked at me like I was a weirdo. I'd often get a response like "this is just the way it is."

Something inside of me never felt at peace with how we were all taught to work and live our lives. I continued to search for answers.

I spent the last number of years learning about myself,

understanding what makes me tick, what makes me happy. Learning what I'm really good at. What are my natural gifts? What do I want for my life? How do I want to live?

Intuitively, I realized it's completely backwards how we pick our careers. We've been taught to pick a career and then mold our lives around it. Why aren't we deciding how we want to live our lives, and then finding a career to support that? So I flipped the traditional method on its head.

I explored what kind of life and lifestyle I wanted and then became determined to figure out what career would support me in achieving it. A career that I absolutely loved. Logically, it made so much more sense to me.

I remember creating a vision board in 2011 and one of the pictures was of a woman on a beach with a laptop. A laptop lifestyle wasn't such a huge thing back then. I had no idea of how I was going to do it, but I knew it was going to happen. I wanted the freedom to be and work anywhere in the world.

I spent years soul-searching and in personal development because I needed to know for sure that the new career I chose would be perfect for me. Being a single parent, I didn't have a back-up person to help with finances. It was all me. I found there were certain pieces I needed to know about myself to figure out the perfect career. No corporate personality assessment was ever going to do the trick.

Once I figured out all the pieces about myself that I

needed to know, the answer just appeared. All of a sudden it became so obvious. I wanted to become a coach. Although in truth, I already was a coach and had been doing it all my life, now it was going to be my profession. It was actually right of me but I just couldn't see it until that moment. It would also provide me the ability to work anywhere in the world. Bingo! In full alignment!

I took a year-long coaching program while working full-time and raising my daughters and then I started my side-business. My plan was to eventually leave corporate, but I was bloody scared. The pressure of being the sole breadwinner of my family was huge. Not to mention the emotional and logistical needs of my daughters fell on me. Most days I felt like I had the weight of the world on my shoulders.

Now, after being fired, I was faced with the reality that all the preparation I had done was now needed in full action.

Although I had bouts of anxiety, I also had many moments of true peace knowing this was exactly where I needed to be. Accompanying this was a deep knowing that nothing in life happens to you, it all happens for you.

Although sometimes it's hard for any of us to see. It's often only in the rear view you can see life's perfection.

Except this time I saw it right away. This wasn't my first rodeo. I could see how this was actually a blessing.

I was already planning my exit strategy from corporate, but was paralyzed in fear.

During this whole time I heard something in my head "you weren't going to move, so we did this for you." I don't know who "we" are, although I've always felt it was a higher intelligence, the universe, whatever you want to call it.

I knew I was being given the most precious gift. The universe knew that I was dragging my feet in taking the leap. They also knew that I would never compromise my personal integrity. This was a no-brainer for this decision to be put on my path. The universe is very sneaky! Damn, it knows what it's doing.

I was being booted out of the nest very unceremoniously!

If the universe thought I was ready to make the full transition, what more could I ever want? It was really time, I just hadn't been ready to see it, yet.

Sometimes, you may see these events as them happening to you, but when crap falls in your lap, the universe knows you are ready. It sees a bigger picture.

You are never given something you can't handle.

I can do this. I can do this. Repeat 100 times daily!

I have been told numerous times that what I did was brave. This has always felt a bit odd to me because it didn't feel brave at all. I didn't even see it as a choice that required any contemplation. If I must choose between honoring myself or not, I choose myself.

I've reflected on why it didn't feel brave. I know there are many people, who, given the same choice, would have gotten the vaccine. However, it doesn't need to be that particular decision. There were many times in my career where I was faced with a choice to do something strongly against my values, or speak my truth. I was an accountant after all. I've seen lots of shifty stuff in corporate that most people don't want to believe is true.

I asked myself…why did I do it so easily?

Firstly, I had a plan. I was already working on an exit strategy. I had been listening to the nudges for many years. I didn't accept hating Mondays and loving Fridays as normal. I listened to my body when it told me that this wasn't right for me.

Our souls are always speaking to us. First our soul speaks to us quietly. It speaks to us in soft whispers like long wild grass rustling in the wind.

"This is not the way."

"There is something not right here."

"THIS, do more of this."

If we don't listen, it gets louder, more insistent. Down right demanding.

Until you're the captain of the Titanic and you've just realized you don't have time to steer the ship away from the iceberg.

I had been listening to those nudges each and every day and responding with the little decisions. When you start with the little decisions, the bigger decisions become a natural progression, and don't feel like a huge leap out of left field.

I knew being a CPA was not the path for me. I had been listening to those nudges, had figured out my next path and had started a side hustle.

Your life begins to open up and you have tons more options when you listen to yourself and take action when you are guided to.

This is where you find true freedom. Nobody can give this to you. It must be something you give yourself permission to do.

Conversely, you paint yourself into a corner when you ignore the nudges and follow a predetermined path on auto-pilot.

I also didn't feel brave because my moments of bravery were long before that event and in moments nobody saw.

I spent hours on my couch when my daughters were with their dad, crying and trying to figure out how to raise them on my own and give them a life I didn't even know how to create.

The very first time I stood up to my employer and put up a boundary and I was trembling on the inside, scared they would fire me on the spot.

It was the thousands of dollars and hundreds of hours I spent in personal development trying to figure out how to change my life when everyone around me told me I was crazy for wanting a better life; how I could never make it on my own.

It was the first time I asked for help when I was raised to believe that asking for help made you weak.

Those were my brave moments. The moments behind closed doors.

It wasn't this moment.

All those times were in preparation for this pivotal point.

I was accustomed to listening to myself. I was used to honoring my soul. I was used to carving my own path. In doing so, I developed a deep sense of inner trust that nobody can break.

The small choices you make each day matter.

There I was, without a job and income. I went from bouts of total freedom and feeling completely liberated to moments of "oh crap, how am I going to make this work?"

I was so glad I had those prior moments of choosing myself to also remember how life goes when you follow your own soul. In the moments of stillness, when I listened to myself, I knew it would all work out.

I discovered that when I choose myself and my own divine path, everything somehow always fell into place. In fact, it doesn't just work out, it usually went in ways I couldn't have ever anticipated. The perfect people, opportunities and situations just fall into my lap.

That is exactly what happened after I was fired. I had made some money in my business while working full-time, but not anywhere near what I needed to maintain my household.

Although I was very confident at coaching, I had not yet determined the steps I needed to run a successful online business at this new scale and magnitude.

True to how life works when you follow the song of your soul, a heart-centered business coach, Jason Moss, landed in my lap. Well, he actually slid into my DM's.

I did what most people don't do in the moment their income dries up and they are flat on their ass. I invested $7K in coaching. It was not the time to shrink back, it was time to expand. He felt like such a blessing and he stood by me in that time, gave me the tools to figure my business out, and even more so, instilled a deeper sense of belief in myself.

I really didn't have the luxury to sit around and figure this out at a leisurely pace. Time is something I have learned to value more than anything in life.

I can't do this journey alone. But at a deeper level, I've also learned that we're not supposed to do it alone. It was never meant to be that way. It's also damn boring doing it alone. If you're not laughing, playing and having fun along the journey, what is the point?

My journey since then has unfolded in the most beautiful way. There were things I expected along the way, but also many things I could not have seen coming.

It's better than I thought it would be. I have met the coolest people, had clients who inspire me to no end, and been blessed to collaborate with the most amazing humans. I've done things I never, ever in a million years thought I could do.

I had strongly felt over the years that it was super unhealthy to become someone you are not, and hide your true essence in your career. However, I had no idea how much life would change when I was now able to completely be my authentic self 24/7. How easy it has become! I realized how much energy I had been using to pretend to be someone I am not. I have watched myself completely blossom into the person I always wanted to be.

Every month I am on this path I become clearer and clearer on what is most important to me. I've also realized that choosing yourself is actually the greatest gift you can give humanity. I am a far happier, more peaceful and loving person than I was when I was a people pleasing rule follower. The more my own heart is overflowing, the more I have to give back.

It was only last year I came across the book, "The 5 Regrets of the Dying" by Bronnie Ware, who worked in palliative care. In that book, she states as the first regret of the dying as "I wish I'd had the courage to live a life true to myself, not the life others expected of me."

This is what I have been working on my whole life. Finding out it was one of the top 5 regrets of the dying has only fueled my mission, not only for myself, but for helping others do the same.

My path has been one of shedding a life and career that I was supposed to, to one that lights my soul on fire.

I am squeezing every juicy bit out of life.

I have way more energy at the end of my work day for my family and people I care about. I have far more patience and love for everything and everyone around me. When my head hits the pillow at night I have a deep sense of inner peace and harmony in my soul and I sleep like a baby. Life is just a shit ton more fun!

Are you squeezing every juicy bit out of life?

If not, are you working on a plan so you don't have to deal with your own HR email moment?

Andrea Horvath is on a mission to empower people to

shift their careers to something that is in
alignment with their souls, so they can squeeze the most
out of life. Her new podcast, "The
Soulful Shift," dives deep into how to shift your career
and life from following what you were
supposed to do, to following the song of your soul.

She operates her own coaching business where she helps
people connect back with themselves,
and become their own guru as they create a career that
supports them and their lifestyle.

Andrea lives in beautiful Vancouver, BC with her two
teenage daughters.

If you are ready to have a career and live a life of limitless
possibilities, that is total alignment
with you, connect with her on LinkedIn:
linkedin.com/in/andreamhorvath or her website:
andreahorvath.com.

REFLECTIONS FROM LIZ & ALAN

Liz Foster
Rattled Awake: Volume Seven

Thanks to my experience with Rattled Awake, I have  since become a contributing writer for a magazine and am currently working on my own book. I am forever grateful for this opportunity and everything it has taught me.

Writing this chapter became a healing journey for me, allowing me to share aspects of myself that I had kept hidden, and it boosted my confidence not only in storytelling but also in my overall writing ability. Facebook: https://www.facebook.com/elizabethfortheloveofself

Alan Chapman
Rattled Awake: Volume Seven

Your new blissful realities are expanding infinitely as you read this. You never knew nor dreamed miracles like these existed, until you were shown. Your soul is yours again: a new way to be, and to show others how.

CRYSTAL BEHE…ALL THAT GLITTERS ISN'T GOLD

Have you ever felt deep betrayal from that friend, family member, "mentor," or colleague you deeply-valued? You were willing to do whatever they asked because they made it out to help you, only to realize later that they only had their interests at heart and were only using you to raise themselves. They would get mad at you when you did better than them or decided to do your own thing without them, making you feel guilty about wanting to do something on your own. Well, I am here to let you know you are not the wrong one, and your true friends and connections want to help you and support you no matter what.

I have often wondered what was wrong with me and why I am not worthy of being loved and respected. I was taught to treat others the way I wanted to be treated, and I took that lesson to heart. I always wanted to belong, wanted to be everyone's friend. It stemmed from being abandoned by my biological mother at six months old and also being raised in the shadow of my older sister, who was the perfect one, a straight-A cheerleader, etc. I wanted to be like her. The problem was I kept trusting the wrong people as they would look all shiny and new, giving me compliments, gifts, etc., only to make fun of me behind my back or toss me aside when I was no longer helpful. When I would go home crying about being bullied by my former friends, my mom would say it was them, not me. They were jealous of me for whatever reason. I didn't believe her at the time and would try to get them to take me back, only to be hurt again and again. I had very low self-esteem my entire life, not that you would know by talking to me.

Growing up, I became a little wiser until I met my ex. He got into my head, making false promises and saying everything I wanted to hear, and I was hungry for love and acceptance. What little self-esteem I had was gradually beaten out of me, literally and figuratively, as he systematically broke me down over nine years. Once I finally got away, I had to lift myself back up. I vowed never to be blinded by false promises and pretty words, only to be fooled repeatedly by people who I thought supported me in my fight to leave him behind altogether. The saying, you find out who your true friends are when you are at your lowest, is very accurate, and sadly, I found that I had very few people I could count on.

So I started over, remolding myself into Crystal Phoenix. I had a mission never to feel silenced again and wanted to help others recover from the trauma of domestic abuse. So, I started networking and making new connections with people I thought supported my mission; most were real, while others were not. The hardest part is that looking back, I could see the signs and, in some cases, was even warned about this person or that one. But I always try to see the best in people, especially when they want to help me.

When I first started as a coach and speaker, I was very unsure; I knew I needed help and wanted to learn all I could about getting my voice heard so that I could make a difference, change the narrative, so to speak, in the domestic abuse awareness community. I wanted to put a stop to victim shaming altogether. So, I started attending and participating in other people's events, whether live events or audio rooms. I got introduced to a group of primarily awesome people and began to grow as a speaker, putting my coaching aside for the time being.

As I grew in confidence, I started to host my audio events called "Life Talks with Crystal Phoenix" and was even invited to be the guest speaker for other people's events. As I started to rise on that platform, I made a few connections. I was excited to be welcomed into this group of people with so much knowledge they seemed willing to share with me. Now looking back, I see it all differently; very reminiscent of the movie Mean Girls.

As I started getting closer to some of them, I learned of deeper cracks in the facade. It happened while I was in the process of writing my first solo book and was battling depression. It was right after the holidays, and I was missing my family. I got a call from the top girl asking me some questions, then telling me she was told not to help me or have me around as I would bring her down. She gave me two different names. I believed her because they had just ended our friendship out of nowhere without even telling me why, (although I have my suspicions.)

I am the type of person who tries to stay out of others' conflicts, not choosing sides when I care about both sides. And when I didn't choose this person over the other, they cut me out—their loss. But by telling me what people were supposedly saying about me, even twisting one person's words (I was given proof of what was said later,) they ingratiated themselves to me. Ingratiating is a psychological technique in which an individual attempts to influence another person by becoming more likable to their target in any number of ways. In this case, they told me they took my side, said they believed in me, and wanted to help me.

Over the next few months, we worked together on many different projects. I learned a lot, and I sang the mean girls' praises for all the help they were giving me, not realizing that they were just using me the whole time. Anytime I would start to pull away from wanting to work on my projects or work with others, they would bring me back by offering me special perks, like spotlights on their shows, helping me learn how to work different programs, etc. In a sense, they were love-bombing me, just not in a romantic way. They were feeding off my energy, and I was happy to support and promote them since I thought they were doing the same for me. Looking back, I have realized that they would only promote me if it benefited them. Whether it was a joint project or they just needed a spot filled, I was more than happy to fill in. I saw it as being able to help others by being heard on other platforms. I felt like I belonged and was finally a part of something bigger than myself and could make a difference.

Then, about a month ago, I started working on a few projects on my own, one of them very important to me. It was so important that I put aside everything to take it on. When I asked for help, I was met with passive aggressive responses. Carrots were dangled before me in promising to make some money with referrals and such. Knowing how money is tight for me, they thought this 'carrot' would bring me back into the fold. Thanks to this 'move' I began to see the truth. As time passed, I started pulling away further until I had a brutal awakening. They very underhandedly tried to discredit the project I was passionate about. That was it for me, my true rattled awake moment.

As I came to the full realization that someone I had come to love and trust as a sister could hurt and betray me in this way, I cried. I felt so betrayed, like being stabbed in the heart while being kissed on the cheek. I went through all of the emotions ranging from hurt, anger and rage, betrayal, and finally, acceptance. The final emotion was the hardest in many ways; I accepted that this person only saw me as a pawn to be used and tossed aside when I didn't do exactly as they wanted. It wasn't my fault for believing they appreciated me as much as I cared and appreciated all they did for me. I was forced to see it for what it was, and accept the many ways glitter faded from my eyes.

I saw what was genuinely happening and that I needed to walk away. As I came to this realization, I began to get scared as we have many of the same connections and friends. Would I lose them all? I had seen what had happened to others, how, once the mean girls decided they didn't like someone they nearly ruined careers. But, as I quietly started to space myself further from them, I began to see that the connections I have made, the real ones that support what I am trying to do, will still be there supporting me like they always have, whether I am supported by the mean girls or not.

I have finally realized that I am enough, and while making solid and lasting connections/friendships in life is essential, whether professionally or privately, at the end of the day, I am enough. I don't need the shiny; I would rather have a small but loyal group of people around me that I can support, and who support me, whether working together or having our own projects. I am always saying that when one of us rises, we all do as we help each other in our endeavors.

I still honestly believe that, in relationships, yes, give and take will always be there, but there is a difference between being genuinely supported, and being used by someone who makes false promises, doing what they can to keep you below them. I want those happy to share the limelight to be true friends. Those are the ones who celebrate your victories and help you back up when you stumble, not caring if they are in the limelight with you or not, letting you enjoy your wins. Your true flock is happy to take turns in the spotlight, not hogging it all, stealing your accomplishments for themselves. Fools gold seeks to turn off the lights. I graduated high school, I don't need to be brought back in with such childish tactics.

I finally feel free of it all.

When you do finally take the steps to walk away and be yourself and acknowledge what happened, you will have to face those who will say you deserved the betrayal, or lash out at you, saying you are ungrateful for all they have done for you. They will say "Don't take it personal, it's just business." I personally hate that, because it is personal when they attack you, even in a passive aggressive manner, not actually saying your name. They are incapable of acknowledging what you have done for them or yourself. They will try to get others to see you as the bad guy painting themselves as the victims. They will try to discredit your feelings or gaslight you trying to make it out like they didn't harm you. Remember not to give in, hold onto your truth, and know that you are entitled to your feelings, embrace them, work through them, learn from what happened so that you can see the red flags when trying to build new relationships. Learn to be observant of how they treat others, because eventually that is how they will treat you. Most importantly, learn to love yourself and be accepting of who you are, that is when you will be able to find your tribe and those who will be the platinum and not fools gold.

People are fickle and can be distracted by what is shiny and new, but at the end of the day, know this: You are the one who matters; you are enough, and it's not your fault for wanting to be a part of something that looks amazing from the outside. My advice to you, which I have to remind myself of all the time, is that you are enough, and when the chips fall, you will know who has your back and who is just fools gold.

It is a lesson I have learned in every type of relationship you can have, and this final time, I finally realized that I don't need to fit in; I just need to be me, and that's enough.

All that glitters isn't gold.

Crystal Behe, also known as Crystal Phoenix, is on a mission to help others rise from the ashes of self-doubt and find their true identity and purpose in life. She has co-authored three international best selling books including "Rattled Awake: Volume Three," where she speaks about her journey recovering from domestic abuse. She has also started her own book series, "Rise of Crystal Phoenix," in which she shares her story of overcoming abuse in many ways. In each part of the series, she breaks down the reasons why victims stay in abusive relationships as long as they do, and provides readers with more awareness of their options. Her intention is to help stop victim shaming and change the way people view survivors. She strives to change the narrative in everything she does.

You can find out more about her at https://www.riseofcrystalphoenix.com or check out her YouTube channel https://www.youtube.com/ @CrystalPhoenix8320

REFLECTIONS FROM
MICH & CRYSTAL

Michelle Laaks art with HeArt

01 July 2024
Rattled Awake hits Vol #10, 2024!

Progress is measured by milestones not measured by the accomplishments of society, but by those of integrity. What is written from the heart becomes the right measure of reference points.

What many good people lack are markers that might tell them how they are actually doing.

Rattled Awake has pivoted into a milestone of volumes more than I could ever have imagined, spring boarding my career opportunities with co-authors and now opening the door to illustrating my third children's book – Yes to 2024! Celebrating a win win for Rattled Awake and for my career.

I have been honoured to have partaken and collaborated together with co-authors in Vol 3 and 5 both hitting International bestsellers #1 in the quickest exposure to my career off-set.

"The best way to predict your future is to create it."
Abraham Lincoln

"Out of difficulties grow miracles." —*Jean de La Bruyère* "

*"A legacy is about leaving your mark on the hearts
of those you love and those you inspire."*

Crystal Behe

As someone who is new to the writing scene Rattled Awake volume 3 and now this very special issue #10 has given me a chance to learn what writing truly is about. I use this series as my guide for what I want to do in my solo series "Rise of Crystal Phoenix" I have learned so much about how to develop my story and get my message across engagingly. I would recommend joining this anthology series to anyone who has something to say and no outlet to say it in.

To learn more about me check out my youtube channel http://www.youtube.com/@CrystalPhoenix8320

SHARON BIRN...DON'T LEAVE YOUR KIDS BEHIND

Have you ever felt like a volcano about to erupt from the pressure of providing financially for your child and wanting to be fully present in their daily life? If you have, you are not alone. I have felt this way multiple times throughout my parenting journey. Quite frankly, there are too many to count.

"I've learned that making a 'living' is not the same thing as making a life." - Maya Angelou

From a very young age, people are primed to think about what they will do with the rest of their lives, their careers, and how they will support themselves. Additionally, there is still a tremendous emphasis on going to college to be successful. Focusing through this lens prepares people to make a living, not make/create a life.

Insidiously, I moved through my young adult life, and some of my adulthood focused on my parents' generational lesson and society's expectations of "making a living" as the determinant of success.

The pressure to 'make a living' intensified after a contentious divorce, instantaneously thrown into the life of a single mom, having to provide for my son financially, physically, and emotionally as both mom and dad amplified the need to make a living.

As a child, one of my favorite songs was *"Cat's in the Cradle"* by Harry Chapin. The lyrics summed up how I was feeling at this time of my life; summed up what I was most afraid of:

> "My child arrived just the other day
> He came to the world in the usual way
> But there were planes to catch and bills to pay
> He learned to walk while I was away
> And he was talking 'fore I knew it, and as he grew
> He'd say, "I'm gonna be like you, Dad.
> You know I'm gonna be like you."

I was forced to find full-time work, which meant before and after-school care for my son. It meant getting to school by 8:30 in the morning and not getting home until almost 6:30 at night, dinner, homework, shower, and bed all to wake up and do it again the next day. We were on automatic pilot, a continual hamster wheel, with no way off. We were getting through daily by going through the motions, surviving, not thriving!

I was doing what I had to do to make a living, either blinded by or strategically ignoring the effects that living a life focused on making a living was having on my son, myself, and our relationship.

My son began getting "sick" frequently, forcing me to take time off, as I had no one who could assist with watching him. On the rare occasions I could find someone to help watch him, he became very resistant to their presence. Overwhelmed by the demands of my everyday life, it felt like the walls were closing in on me. Patience, time, and energy were things that I used to feel like I had an abundance of; however, that had all changed instantaneously. I began to respond like a pressure cooker under too much pressure.

We often spend our lives in hurry-up mode, like in the game show Beat the Clock. My son naturally took things more slowly and was taking things even more slowly to have more time with me. Sadly, I had tunnel vision of my responsibilities and did not see what his behavior told me. I now realize his behavior told me, Mom, I need you. I need you to be present with me.

His behavior was crying out, I miss you, Mom. I miss the days when I would get upset and angry when you would diffuse my anger by playing tickle tag. That was the game of tag we are all familiar with, except when you caught someone, you didn't tag them, you tickled them.

I want to go back to singing and dancing with you, Mom. We need to play video games. Mario Brothers tournament, Mortal Kombat, Pokemon.

At nine years old, he was diagnosed with anxiety. It was so severe that he had school avoidance. Many days, he had school refusal: He would lock himself in the bathroom, and NOT come out to go to school, no matter what I did or said. Internally, this put me into a tailspin. How would I continue to make a living and provide for us when I couldn't, nor would I leave my nine-year-old home alone? Finding people who could or would help was nearly impossible because of their schedules and my son's resistance to having anybody around but me.

I experienced a myriad of emotions and, at the same time, continued to fight a daily battle to either get him to go to school or find someone who could watch him so that I could successfully get to work. I was sad, hurting, angry, frustrated, feeling like a failure, feeling guilty—the list goes on and on. Every day, my heart was splitting into a million pieces.

There's nothing I want more in my life than to help others and to be a mom. While there is never a perfect balance of 50/50, the scales were so lopsided by the feeling of having to choose to sacrifice the values that were very important to me: family first above all else.

This tug of war, both internal and external, went on for years. My son continued to communicate with me through his behavior. Although he is very intelligent and articulate, he would shut down, communicating mostly through inaction.

Frustrated and heartbroken by the fact that I was being asked to choose between having a job that I was born to do and being a mom, I would frequently cry myself to sleep or cry on my way to work. I secretly struggled with the desire to "have it all" and felt like I wanted to put my head through a wall. I couldn't figure out how to have it all. I was convinced there had to be a way for me to have a meaningful career helping others while being able to support myself and my son. And still, be able to be the mom that I wanted to be: The mom who was present, the mom who was able to, more times than not, put her child's needs before anything else, spending quality time and making quality connections.

> "Too many times, we stand aside.
> And let the waters slip away.
> 'Til what we put off 'til tomorrow
> Has now become today
> So don't you sit upon the shoreline
> And say you're satisfied
> Choose to chance the rapids
> And dare to dance the tide."
> Garth Brooks "The River"

Years of criticism, judgment, blame, and unsolicited advice from my ex-husband, parents, friends, and school personnel, kept me pushing to "get to work" and provide. Extremely high cholesterol, high blood sugar, and high blood pressure were indicators that the life I was living was sending me down a path that was not healthy, and with potentially irreversible consequences, and yet I continued to bury my head like an ostrich in the sand.

The mic drop moment, the moment I got rattled awake to my core, was when my son said. with tears running down his face, "Mom, I need you!" for the 15th time in that month of not wanting to leave my side for school. He begged for both of us to stay home just for one day of quality time.

At that moment, I stopped dead in my tracks. Time stood

still. As I hugged him I thought to myself fuck this. Enough is enough.

I knew I had to make changes immediately. My son's behavior was, and now his words, like a stake through my heart, were telling me change must happen now. Who would teach my son the values that I so desperately wanted him to learn? Who would nurture his beautiful, unique soul? The answer was ME that's who. I would never again let him feel that anything was more important than he was to me.

Rattled awake by the realization that making a 'living' is not the same thing as making a life, I wanted to make/ create a life that both my son and I would love. The legacy I have left behind is far more important than the amount of money left in my bank account when I depart from Earth. My son is the greatest legacy I will ever leave. I want to be remembered for who I was and for the effort and attention I put into cultivating my son to reach his full potential. I want to be remembered for having a hand in honoring the greatest gift. I was given the opportunity to help mold another human being into their version of greatness.
Does any of this resonate with you?

I was determined not to sacrifice my son's well-being as it has always been and still is my greatest priority. I knew what I had to do; the truth is I had no idea how I was going to do it.

"There's bound to be rough waters
And I know I'll take some falls

> But with the good Lord as my captain
> I can make it through them all."
> Garth Brooks, "The River"

I had to find a way to provide for my son financially and be fully present in his daily life. This is what he was used to; it had always been something I had always told myself I would do, which is to be fully present and make my children's emotional well-being of paramount importance. How often have you promised yourself that your child's emotional well-being would come first, only to be disappointed when you could not make that happen?

It was time to create a life, That would allow me to be present, and bring inner peace to both my son and myself.

> "You know a dream is like a river
> Ever changin' as it flows
> And the dreamer's just a vessel
> That must follow where it goes
> Trying to learn from what's behind you
> And never knowing what's in store
> Makes each day a constant battle
> Just to stay between the shores."
> Garth Brooks, "The River"

I was on a mission to craft a life that would allow me to fulfill my responsibilities as a parent, while simultaneously creating opportunities for our continued connection. It was time to implement a strategy I now refer to as choose to infuse: Infuse opportunities to get tasks done and have quality time, all in one.

This determination evolved into us doing everyday tasks together, and lent itself to my teaching him skills and building the character traits he would need to be a well-adjusted successful human being. But it was so much more…

Who would have thought that I would have given playing video games, Pokemon, and becoming a fan of Korean pop music, priority status? Not me, for sure; I hated playing video games. I was never any good at them. My turns lasted 0-to-3 seconds before getting killed. Trust me when I tell you that has not changed one bit from my childhood to now. It got to the point where my son finally became comfortable with saying, "Mom, you can just watch while I play, because when I play with you, it's like I'm playing by myself anyway." To play with him or watch him play, I would tell him I first had to get the laundry done, the kitchen clean, or start preparing dinner. He could help me complete the tasks so they would get done quicker, or he could play by himself until I was done. At times, he would choose the latter, stamping his feet or asking me every five minutes or less if I was done. When I would tell him no, I was not, he would scream or cry, just leave it and come play with me. At times, he would pull on my heartstrings enough I would do exactly that. However, on other occasions, I would tell him that when I'm done, I am all yours. Sometimes, he would protest by sitting on the couch, continuing to stamp his feet as he continued to play.

There was a third outcome, and this, to my surprise

initially, happened most often. He would get up and come help me speed up what he called my extremely slow pace of getting things done. He often joked, "You're doing this on purpose because you don't like playing video games, and you get bored with just watching!"

I love all kinds of music but I had no clue that I would truly learn to enjoy and love Korean pop music. I have my son to thank because he not only taught me the names of the groups, he insisted I learn the names of every member of these groups and remember which groups each member was in. Trust me when I tell you it was not an easy feat, but one I am very proud of to this day. Truth be told, I don't understand Korean, but I do love the melodies, and most importantly, I love to see the smile and the joy that singing these songs, and dancing the very intricate choreography, brings to my son's face.

Korean pop music became the background for all the things we did together. We would cook his dinner favorites, homemade mac and cheese, cheese tortellini with homemade sauce, spaghetti and meatballs, cheese ravioli, and chicken parmesan, all to the beat of K-Pop. As you can probably tell, my son has a discerning palate. If you notice a theme, you are correct: homemade sauce and pasta are staples for him. Pasta, well, that's its own food group. Clothes went into the laundry machine in step with the choreography he learned; food got stirred, all as we danced.

Korean pop music became the background while I was working and my son was doing homework. It also became the music we sang along with, and chair-danced to at red lights when driving together in the car.

"Twice" was the first group he ever introduced me to. As I think back on them now, I laugh: we didn't listen to them just twice, we listened to them twice times infinity. Singing along to lyrics without knowing the words prompted prayers that nothing offensive would ever come out of my mouth. I hoped nobody would start a fight or clock me. I would sing these songs throughout my day, smiling as wide as the ocean, immediately transported back to home, where my son and I were completing tasks together while being serenaded, twice.

Henry Ford was quoted as saying "If you think you can't you're right, if you think you can, you're right." So, if you think you can't provide for your child financially as well as be truly present in their daily life you are right. Conversely, if you think you can provide for your child financially and be present truly in their daily life, you are right!

Seek ways to be present. I spoke to my boss and got permission to bring work home and or work extra hours in a day so that I would be able to take Flex hours on another day to attend events at my son's school. It might be possible for you, too.

Excerpt, Harry Chapin's "Cats in the Cradle"

"I called him up just the other day
I said I'd like to see you if you don't mind
He said, I'd love to, Dad, if I can find the time
You see, my new job's a hassle, and the kids have the flu

But it's sure nice talking to you, dad
It's been sure nice talking to you
And as I hung up the phone, it occurred to me
He'd grown up just like me
My boy was just like me
And the cat's in the cradle, and the silver spoon
Little boy blue and the man in the moon
"When are you coming home, son?" "I don't know when"
But we'll get together then, Dad
We're gonna have a good time then."

Consider it a compliment that your son is just like you. I do. Sensitive, Passionate, funny, and sarcastic... warms my heart like a campfire to marshmallows and creates a spontaneous smile as bright as the sun and as big as the Earth! I think to myself, yes, my boy is just like me! You can have it too!

Sharon is a world-renowned life coach, international number one best-selling co-author, and public speaker. She helps moms and their children beat burnout, enabling them to thrive. As a single mom to her son and a dog mom to Minnie, Sharon understands the challenges and joys of family life.

Her speaking engagements are highly sought after,

covering crucial topics such as effective communication, addressing special needs, and the importance of quality family time. In her anthology contribution, Sharon shares a personal experience that "rattled her awake," shaping her approach to life and family. She emphasizes taking time away from the daily grind to recharge, allowing parents and children to become their best versions.

Sharon's mission is to return the fun to family time, encouraging deep connections and lasting memories. Her unique blend of personal and professional wisdom makes her an inspiring and influential figure in family well-being.
https://www.linkedin.com/in/sharon-birn-9a4a5792/
http://www.possibilitiesrinfinite.com

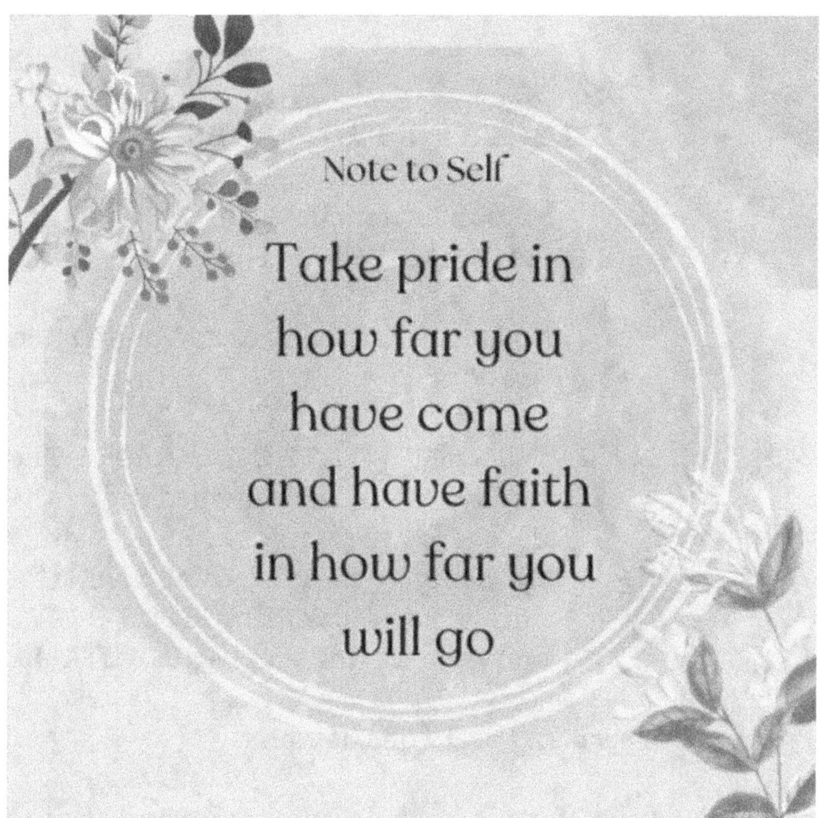
Note to Self

Take pride in
how far you
have come
and have faith
in how far you
will go

REFLECTIONS FROM ROBB

Robb Profancik
Rattled Awake: Volume Five

To all the Rattled Awake: Volume Ten Authors:

WELCOME TO THE FAMILY!!!! The family where we emerged from the darkness...the trauma...the despair... By being a part of this wonderful family, you are COURAGEOUS, BRAVE and portraying an INDOMITABLE spirit!!!
I'm proud of each and every one of you!

"Rattled Awake" for me, was definitely a major healing point in my journey. It gave me the opportunity to spread my story to others and let them know they are not alone. It also gave me extra confidence in knowing I never want to return to that darkness ever again.
Whatever our story is...we have a duty to share it and give others hope for a brighter tomorrow!
I wish you all Peace, Love and Happiness!
Robb Profancik - Machine Assembler at Kiffer Industries Inc - Kiffer Industries Inc | LinkedIn

MEGAN GAITHER...THE REAL MEGAN GAITHER STORY

October 2023

A knock at my classroom door on a Monday morning during lunch was unexpected but not unusual. Teens liked to skip lunch and wander the high school halls anytime they were able, often pestering the teachers they trust within their rooms. Tap, tap, tap. I slowly stood up from my desk and meandered to the door. Through the door's window, no one peered back at me as I checked to see who knocked. Now this seemed unusual... I pushed the door open, thinking I must catch whoever left before they walked out of sight, and a piece of paper, folded neatly in quarters, dropped suddenly to the ground. I bent to pick it up and brought it into my room, letting the door slam shut behind me. The paper read, "We know your secret... Ava." My first thought: who's Ava? I tried to recall if I had any students by this name, but I couldn't, so I called my best friend.

I read the note to her, and chuckled, "What secret do they think they know, and who's Ava?" She paused and became apprehensive.

"You were, Megan."

It all hit me like a train, hard, heavy, and with a finality I felt even then, before my administrative leave began. I was Ava. How did they find out?

"Whenever you feel yourself criticizing any one...
just remember that all the people in the world
haven't had the advantages you've had..."

-F. Scott Fitzgerald

People make mistakes; sometimes life altering ones. But not everyone has their mistakes and personal life made public to the world. My fourth year teaching, I was beginning to feel confident; I was thriving: I knew my worth and my data from the testing scores; I felt like I belonged in the school, the community in which I grew up, and in the district. I didn't realize the choice I made over the summer would come back to haunt me as I finished the 2023 football season. The criticism I faced for the choices I made only fueled my bitterness and hatred for the school and the media, but it was the public scrutiny which impacted my mental health the most. Not everyone could understand the harm they cause behind a keyboard, but faced with the same level of hatred I endured, it would break them down, too. I wouldn't wish this pain on anyone, even those people who were most vocal during my tragedy.

Flashback to the summer of 2023

On a random Tuesday in May, I hit submit on my last essay assignment for my second master's degree. It was almost anticlimactic... I worked so hard, and I cried so many tears for this moment of finality. I didn't want to walk the stage. Arizona State was too far away from my home for that, plus I did it two years prior already. But this... this degree encapsulated the dream I had been waiting for; the one giving the most pride to have achieved. So, hitting submit, knowing I completed the course load felt surreal. However, along with my pride in myself comes a looming dread... I'd been in college for over a decade now, taking out student loans to fund my education. Those debts would be coming due, sooner than I anticipated. I was on a teacher's salary, and not only that, I was on a teacher's salary in Missouri. Missouri is ranked 50th in the nation, proving our teachers make less than any other teacher in the United States. To make matters worse, I taught in one of the poorest school districts around the area. I couldn't afford the $1,000 or more they charged me each month, not even in a dual income household.

This revelation inspired my husband and I to make a unique decision, and one that would likely be fun as well as financially smart. I started an Only Fans content creator page to help save money over the summer to hopefully pay our bills when they came due during the school year. I knew the consequences of this choice, should I get caught, but I tricked myself into the belief that I would be smart: I used a pseudonym, Paige Preslee, and showed no facial features in any content or pictures. "No face, no case."

This summer, I blossomed into a more confident and healthier version of myself using Only Fans as a catalyst to inspire me. It's fun; I loved doing it. I've met some great people, and I don't want to stop, so I don't. I continue, albeit much more slowly, into the first month of the school year. As head cheer coach and the advanced courses English teacher, the continuation of Only Fans slowed to a glacial pace to enable me to be successful at the job I loved most: teaching. However, the content creation led me to my identity development. Quitting cold turkey proved harder than expected.

About That Note...

I hung up the phone, not knowing what to do next, so I decided to do what I would have done anyway: teach. Fourth hour was my plan period, so I used it to panic. I knew what this note meant for me. If the district didn't know yet, they will very soon, and once they know, I would have the same treatment as my best friend from the previous month. It's just a matter of time before my worst nightmare from the summer comes true. If not today, tomorrow the school will be investigating my personal, online presence.

I told myself, *the only good thing is it's all gone.* All evidence of Only Fans has been deleted. I figured the school would put me on leave to investigate, but since there's nothing out there, they'll let me come back.

The rest of Monday became a blur of panic. I pretended nothing was wrong, but deep down, I knew the student body circulated the rumors. I taught my lessons that day with my mind racing against the clock. What did I need to do before my leave meeting? How could I make this transition easier for my colleagues, so they won't struggle until I come back? Wishful and delusional thinking had me in a chokehold. Teachers don't come back from allegations of doing porn in their free time, but my identity entangled with my job. I couldn't fathom the true outcome of that single note left on my door at eleven in the morning.

End of September 2023

My friend's demise at the school became very public and gained international notoriety. It prompted discussions about what was expected from teachers and the appalling statistics on teacher pay in the United States. It was big news heard around the world, prompting headlines in places such as Europe, Latin America, and Australia. My friend decided to make the best of her situation, but I had opposing feelings. I was determined to keep my job teaching, so I made the hardest choice I had yet to make in life. Delete my Only Fans account or keep it?

It's Wednesday: early dismissal for the students and professional development for the remainder of contractual hours for the teachers. As I sat at my desk for a few minutes to collect myself after my rowdy seventh hour ended, I received a text: "I think I'm being fired."

I texted her back, "What? What's happening?"

Silence.

I called her.

No response.

I grabbed my notebook for the whole staff meeting but made my way down the hall to my friend's classroom. Before I make it halfway, I am stopped.

"Megan, I think she's in a meeting and won't make it in time for our meeting. Come to the library."

During the meeting, I didn't hear a word my principal said. I worried and panicked inside. I knew why she was called into this meeting… I knew the danger this put me in. My friend's Only Fans was found. She would be fired, and if I'm not careful, I'd be next. In a state of terror, I deleted my Only Fans and X accounts while I sat in my Jeep Wrangler in the school parking lot. The weeks that followed blurred with panic. I loved teaching my students and coaching. I didn't want to lose it, but I'm so close to my friend. I knew I'd be perceived as guilty.

Two highly respected colleagues of mine stopped me one day, the same week my friend was put on administrative leave. "You have two of us in your corner… Keep your head down and do your job. Do it well. You are being watched and are 'guilty by association' of what your friend has done. Just know we know who you are and how good you are for students, and we have your back."

These colleagues were among the very few to continue to talk to me and treat me like a person during the month that followed. I was an outcast; I was 'mean girled.' The people around me pulled away, so much so that they wouldn't even sit at the same table as me. Many women would get up and move if I sat down at the same table to eat or tried to be a part of their group and conversation. I was tiptoed around. No one would speak to me unless it was required of them. I felt the cold shoulder everywhere I went. This caused extreme stress and sadness, leaving me in tears each night as I left the building and drove home. The job I loved turned into a nightmare for me. How could I fix this?

Spoiler: I couldn't.

> "They slammed the door on my whole world.
> The one thing I wanted." -Taylor Swift

That note in my door kicked off a week of torture for me; one that left me with trauma I will likely cope with for years in therapy. Not only was I expected to perform all my duties that week, but I was treated like an outcast. Administration pretended nothing was going on, even though I had a documented history of anxiety and panic attacks due to the stress and trauma of school-related issues. My life and my career were now an after thought because of one picture that appeared on social media: a picture I didn't even consent to have posted.

Halloween 2023

Friday, the day I planned for weeks! My assistant coach was assigned to this game, so I could enjoy a costume party with my friend. We shared our duties as coaches for cheerleading season, a fact well known by administration. After all, it was the whole reason we advocated to add her position to our cheerleading team.

Cheer is a sport that lasts from August through March, not including the pressure of tryouts in May and summer-long practices and events. It is a sport that needs to give its coaches periodic breaks, so we did it! We advocated and were granted our request after gathering information and data and meeting with the activities director and the school superintendent in 2022.

My assistant coach worked for me, and I attended a costume party in honor of Halloween with my best friend. I bought a costume and left for the party in east St. Louis. The party roared! It featured a complete hotel takeover with a shuttle to a local venue for dancing and drinks. I walked around, quiet and head down, because I realized I only knew one person there; I felt bashful. My friend and I danced and had some drinks to loosen up my nerves. The music was deafening: a hiphop beat mixed with a song I didn't recognize, and I realized I'm having so much fun! I swayed to the beat, sipping on my vodka-cranberry, and I felt the tension leech from my body. Before long, the bar closed. It was time to take the last pictures and head back to the hotel. I stood in front of the neon angel wings against the wall and my friend and I took selfies. Then, a couple of women approached and asked to take a picture of us. My friend was newly famous, so we stood together and took this single picture before heading back to our hotel.

The hotel was quiet. We are in the "overflow" hotel since the party hotel sold out of its rooms. My friend needed to work, creating content in a livestream. I fluffed my hair and blotted my face as she discussed the plan for her livestream.

"Megan, do you want to be a featured guest in my live show?"

I missed doing my own content, so this opportunity might be a good way to feel like I'm a part of it again... Thirty minutes later, my friend called me into the shot. I was only in it for a few minutes, so we needed to make it count for her. I slid into the frame as she blocked the camera view so I could get into position. The camera would only see me from the back, so my identity was safe from people who might recognize me. I didn't want to be caught; I loved my job as a teacher and coach, but I did notice the absence of not continuing to create content and the connections I made with so many people on Only Fans. This livestream gave me one last taste of what I lost already: my account and the people I met while doing it.

So, my friend called out to me, "I have a special friend; one I just met today, and she is going to help me... Ava?"

I walked to the edge of the frame as she knelt in front of the camera to hide any glimpses the viewers might have. Crawling into position, I wiggled to entice the viewers, my long, black hair cascading down my back. My friend and I performed for a few minutes until she told me to make my way out of frame again. She finished her livestream with just enough time to make it back to the room crawl at the main hotel. That night was a blur of dancing and music until I woke up and returned to my normal life once again.

To my surprise, those few minutes on camera, along with the angel wings photo, led to my tragic downfall. That weekend, a local photography company posted my photo on the social media platform called X with my face blurred out, standing next to my friend. Monday morning, at lunch, a note slipped into the crevice of my door.

The consequences of one's actions...

The picture posted on X, paired with the few minutes of my guest appearance in a livestream, sparked controversy within my school community. Everyone knew what was happening to me, but no one talked to me about it. I felt stuck in a constant state of terror and dread for the entirety of the week, causing my panic disorder to make me have panic attacks multiple times a day. However, I was supposed to be a professional. I couldn't show weakness, so I continued teaching and created lesson plans for the inevitable administrative leave that loomed over my head.

The worst day of the week...

Tuesday arrived. Students each hour began to be pulled from their classes, including mine, and interrogated by school administration and guidance counselors. Many students came back to me, telling me in horror what they were being asked about me. They were asked if they knew where I was Friday night, if the picture was without a doubt me, if I had ever said anything to them about Only Fans, and so many more leading questions. They were asked if I was ever inappropriate with them or had inappropriate conversations. Fortunately for me, most of my students were honest and said of course not, one even going so far as to say, "What you are doing to Ms. Gaither is bullshit, and I refuse to answer any of these questions." I'm forever grateful for their honesty. Unfortunately for me, a couple students and cheerleaders who weren't fond of me decided to advocate for my removal after school ended. They could be heard in the office saying, "Why is she still here? Why hasn't she been fired yet?" I did not expect it out of this group of girls, whom I taught the entire previous year in my honors course, and was teaching in my dual credit course. We had a rewarding and professional relationship until this point, so I felt a lot of pain hearing about this turn of events. Some students went so far as to tell the school district lies, such as me admitting and bragging about having an Only Fans.

As an adult professional, I know that was career suicide; it simply was false. They stated I was a bad coach, failing to provide coaching instruction, all of which I denied and will continue to deny vehemently.

Tuesday was full of delusions, yet, it was also the day I decided to prepare for my inevitable period of leave. Because my friend was put on hers on a Wednesday early-out, I figured I had two days to get ready for my substitute teacher. Hopefully, I could come back after it was over. Hope kept me going; hope kept me typing lesson plans rather than saving my curriculum materials I spent years and many unpaid hours creating. I now regret this act of kindness. I hoped the school would see the value I brought to the district and would allow me to come back once the investigation was completed. I was wrong. They chose not to see their nose to spite their face.

My department head visited my classroom today to see how I was holding up. He was the only teacher to extend any kindness to me during this week and treat me like I wasn't a pariah. He asked if I knew what was happening and what the rumors were, so I was honest and told him yes. I told him I was gathering lesson plans and materials to make the transition smoother for my substitute, but I had every intention of coming back. I regret this lie, even though I made it out of love and a good place. I should have known I was not coming back. Teachers don't easily make a comeback after any period of leave is forced upon them. I haven't spoken to him personally since, and I worry about him hating me for leaving my classroom and position, even though I did not want to leave. I worried about the lessons after my plans were completed being forced onto him to make and see through. I still hope he sees me as the teacher I was, not the harlot I've been made out to be.

It should be over today… right?

Wednesday: the day of anticipated dread. The day continued as it did that week: students continually pulled out of my classroom, interrogations about myself as a person, teacher, and as a coach. A member of administration came to my classroom during 2nd period to check up on me and make sure I was doing my job as a teacher. He found me sitting with my cheerleading captains, discussing a possible fundraiser, with a phone in my hand. I was texting my assistant coach as we discussed ideas to make the cheerleading savings account in the positive again. After purchasing needed items for our athletes, we realized we were negative and needed to rectify that immediately. However, no questions were asked; nothing spoken. He departed after a minute in the room. During my fourth hour plan period, another member of administration visited me. That meeting is not documented formally and lasted much longer than the observation prior to it. *This conversation serves no purpose,* I thought. It's simply the school district trying to cover themselves, but no formal discipline was established.

"Megan, I'm just checking in with you about a few things. The assistant principal noticed you on your phone today during class. Have you been on your phone more than normal recently?"

"Recently? I'd say yes. With what is going on here, I need to calm myself by messaging my people and keeping my mind busy."

"What is going on? Do you need to talk about something?"

"If that's how you are going to play this, I guess I'll say nothing is going on and leave it at that."

"Megan, I just want to make sure you are the great teacher I know you to be. Are you having trouble in your personal life? I heard you are getting divorced."

"I am separated from my husband. It is a hard time for me."

"Well, you know that divorce is hard on children. You really should consider that."

The conversation made me extremely uncomfortable and did nothing to acknowledge the investigation that was occurring while I was teaching this week. I still struggle with the unprofessionalism, the invasive line of questioning, and lack of sympathy at the hands of the administration this week.

The end of the school day arrived with much of the same occurring, but I made it to the end. I thought, *the end comes quickly for me and the torture will stop.* My friend was put on leave during the early out meeting. I wondered if the same would happen to me. I waited in my room for what seemed like ages but in reality fifteen minutes passed, and the English department meeting began imminently. I made my way to the department head's classroom and led the sophomore and junior level data and assessment-based meeting. Administration visits and listens to our meeting, but my torture doesn't end. I go home. I cry. I decide I cannot deal with another day of torment, so I call in sick for mental health reasons for Thursday.

The uneventful Thursday passes quickly. Near the end of the school day, the activities director called. The first kindness and care I receive comes from him.

"First off, are you okay? How are you doing?"

"Well, I've been better."

"I understand that… I'm calling to see if you are planning on attending the game tomorrow night."

"Of course. I just needed a day away from it all. I'll be there tomorrow."

Thursday spelled the end of my career as a teacher and began the public scrutiny when a reporter from the St. Louis Post Dispatch called me for a statement. "Multiple" colleagues called them to say another teacher allegedly has an Only Fans account. They wanted my statement. I was given less than twelve hours to make a statement or not.

"If I don't say anything, since I'm not even on leave

currently, will you still run this story?"

"Unfortunately, the story will run regardless. We'll just use what your colleagues have told us. The story is too big in light of what happened to your friend last month."

So, I chose to give myself a voice. With something like porn out in the media, a career is already over. I told them my story, from beginning in May 2023 until that day, including how my Only Fans career ended officially when my friend was caught. I told him how much teaching meant to me and how I would give up all the money I earned, or would earn, to keep my career as a teacher, but the damage is done. The one request the media granted me was they would hold the story until after the football game the next day. I didn't want my cheerleaders to miss their game because their coach was asked to leave.

Regret: my life summed up in one word *at this point.* Actions have consequences, and I have to live with mine. I knew what was coming. The media's portrayal of me, people's perceptions of me, the criticism and backlash I would face, and, of course, the administrative leave, which still hadn't been discussed with me at this point, but I knew it was coming. What I didn't know was that unlike my friend, the district was trying to pin other accusations on me to scare me into leaving on my own.

Gameday!

Usually an exciting experience, but this one for me was nauseating. The anxiety of going to the game, when word was already spreading around the school and the community, felt like a waking nightmare, but I prepared myself mentally to accomplish this one last task. However, around three in the afternoon, a member of administration called me and requested a meeting before I spoke with any of my cheerleaders at the game. We agreed to meet at five; I understood what was coming, and I knew I would never speak to my team again in a coaching capacity. It hurt. I cried and screamed, but I pulled my shit together, and I went to that meeting with my head held high.

The meeting involved two administrators: one asking leading and accusatory questions and then telling me "that's not what we heard" when I answered, and one who took notes quietly. The meeting involved lines of questioning including how I communicate with students (email and the district approved Remind application), conversations we have had about my personal life (a separation), and why I didn't go to the game the previous Friday. After the questioning was over, they told me I would be placed on paid administrative leave, pending an investigation into the allegations, and requested my keys. I left the building and immediately contacted the news and told them to release the story at seven pm, right when the game began.

Three weeks of public persecution followed before the results of the investigation came forward. A supposed eight page document of wrongdoing on my part accumulated in the request for me to resign, as my friend had. However, myself, my teacher's union and their lawyer were never granted access to this document. In fact, No formal list of "charges" has ever been granted to me. I refused to resign; instead, I chose to wait, in favor of allowing the school to make the move as to firing me, if such was their option. I would have chosen to fight, if that were the case. The fact is, they violated my rights and their own policies during my extended leave. However, my depression at the loss of my dream job prevented me from taking action. Instead, I chose to take the leave, the benefits, and the salary as was owed to me by the district, according to the contract we both signed.

> "Hope is not found in a way out but a
> way through." -Robert Frost

I chose to sit in my discomfort, seeking solace in therapy, medication, and those who supported and loved me through the worst experience of my life. I chose to suffer my way through, in hopes of seeing a light at the end of the tunnel.

I remained on paid leave through the 2023-2024 school year. The school elected to pay my full contract from October to the present simply because the allegations they chose to pin on me were not enough to fire me; no hard proof was able to be found.

I learned a lot about myself and my identity through this experience. Like anyone who loses their beloved career, I wondered what was going to happen to me next, what my future career prospects looked like as a well-educated woman working in the adult industry, and how I would get past the betrayal I felt at the school. As T.S. Eliot once said, *"Only those who will risk going too far can possibly find out how far one can go."*

This chapter is the beginning of me taking back ownership of my life.

Grief consumes you if you let it, and I did (am) grieving the loss of something which meant the world to me. I went through all of the stages, albeit maybe not in order and with a lot of back and forth between them. I bargained for my job back and for a chance to have a do over. But that's not how life works. Afterall, you "can't repeat the past" (F. Scott Fitzgerald.) But like Jay Gatsby in my favorite novel, I wished for another chance. I had hope that it all would work out for me. When that chance never came, I became depressed, angry, and bitter, all in one. I don't think I will ever truly forgive the school district for how they treated a once well-respected member of the school and community, and I wish I could say I've accepted my fate and moved on from the experience. For me, it is still ongoing. I'm still in the midst of it; I only began this journey eight months ago. I still have a lot of healing, introspection, and work to do to make my dreams come true for the second time.

How did one individual move forward?

At the end of October when I was caught, a common question I received was "What's next for you? What will you do for work?" I said from the beginning I will advocate; first, I believed I could only advocate for teachers and education. However, I now understand that this experience can speak to all people going through a major life or career transition, especially those who already feel like it's too late to start over… It's not too late, and we can be successful, even later in life when it seems impossible. I will write books and speak out against not only the treatment of teachers, but for others as well. I will make this experience matter, and I can tell you, my small town won't soon forget my name. I matter, you matter, and this experience will be worth all the pain and heartache I went through. The transition I began when my world collapsed around me may be an extreme example, but I hope to inspire others going through major life changes and tell them their world doesn't end when one door is slammed shut on them; it is just beginning.

Megan Gaither is on a mission to advocate for real life change transitions, discuss hard topics of public scrutiny and how to cope with the mental health crisis that comes with such transitions and criticism. She has two master's degrees: a Master of Arts in Teaching from Missouri Baptist University and a Master of Arts in English from Arizona State University.

After receiving her education, Megan wished to make a difference in the lives of adolescents and became a high school English teacher. She also is a mother of two boys, aged almost 9 and 6.

Megan is on a personal mission to reclaim her power and her life after a public and traumatic leave from education. She is an author, Only Fans content creator, and a public speaker who has a gift for connecting with others.

Connect with her here:

X: @megangaither (x.com/megangaither)

Instagram: @megan.gaither92

Instagram.com/megan.gaither92

LinkedIn

REFLECTIONS FROM GREG

Greg Spiller: "What Happened To My Internet?" Rattled Awake VOL 7

I had a wonderful experience working with the eclectic group of writers for VOL Seven. It was a great on-ramp into being a published writer for the first time; a single chapter of a story without the pressure of an entire book.

I told my story in a technical way, about a cosmic phenomenon that impacts our daily lives, and shared important information to be prepared for the worst case scenario. Handy information meant to be accessible and concise for all.

I am incredibly honored to be a part of the rattled Awake anthology series, and proud to be amongst the group of writers that have come forth to share their own journey and unite in speaking to the masses of the moments awakening us all....
Greg on LinkedIn

NANCY O'NEILL...THE IMPACTS OF UNSEEN, INVISIBLE BRAIN TRAUMA

Living for so many years feeling unsure of my future, becoming an educator, being the best mom I could be, holding a broken relationship together enduring endless suffering at times. How did I find the will to keep going? Coming from a broken home at the age of 14, my mother struggled with Bi Polar disorder and my older sister was diagnosed at age 16 with the same disorder. Both of them were experiencing grave hardships, me trying to hold everything together. My father, at the time, was a hard working functional alcoholic who eventually gave up, not able to hold his shit together. He left and I had to pick up the pieces. I had to grow up fast. I didn't know as a child about implied trauma; hell we didn't even know what that word was, not in my home, and it wasn't really taught in school. Not until I started dating, wow what a game that was at times. I recommend that if you are a parent encourage your children not to date until they are mature enough to make rational decisions. I know it has heavily influenced my life and could have been my downfall. There is no need to date early, live some first, find out who you are and finish your education.

"The only thing standing between you and outrageous success is continuous progress."
—Dan Waldschmidt

"Success is no accident. It is hard work, perseverance, learning, studying, sacrifice and most of all, love of what you are doing or learning to do." —Pelé

As I lay here wondering, where should I go, what should I do? Some days it's a struggle to pull my head from my pillow. I want to cry, laugh, scream, run in a whole new direction. Finding and exposing the truth hidden within society is not always that easy. You must work hard, take the blows, be flexible and efficient.

Not coming from a rich family, you have two choices: work for what you want or live poor, always wanting more. I choose to put my best foot forward and keep reaching to obtain my goals. No one can do the work for me. It can be down right difficult, almost self defeating.

What's in your heart? A will to survive? For me, there is no other way. I encourage those of you who are struggling, I encourage you to seek help, ask questions and find support wherever possible. You matter and your mental health is vital!

Not until I started dating, (wow what a game that was at times), did I put two -and-two together. From where I sit now, I recommend that if you are a parent, encourage your children not to date until they are mature enough to make rational decisions. I know it has heavily influenced my life and could have been my downfall. There is no need to date early, live some first, find out who you are and finish your education.

Directly out of university on the Rez, I married a man struggling with alcohol abuse. I didn't know he had massive trauma hidden inside of him. Geez, I felt like he swore at me everyday. I remember running away very fast, fleeing in my vehicle to get away from the verbal abuse. Hours of it, weeks, months which led to years. I'm tough so I learned to fight back. If he swore at me I would swear back. I remember one time early in our marriage, before my first son was born. We were arguing and wrestling over a loaded shotgun on the floor. His parents lived just across the way and his mom called the RCMP (Royal Canadian Mountain Police.) Boy, we had to scramble to come out of our battle or he would have gone to jail. Isn't it crazy what we will do to protect those we think we are in love with? It was hardly the place for a young lady trying to hold it all together with no support. How could I have known this was part of my journey and the suffering was necessary? This led me to who I am today. The lessons I have experienced cannot go untold.

"Character cannot be developed in ease and quiet. Only through experience of trial and suffering can the soul be strengthened, vision cleared, ambition inspired and success achieved."   —Helen Keller

My trauma made me stronger. It was the reason for tough decisions in my life. Once I had my son, I knew I had to break free of that environment. Wow, when you are inside of those scary relationships you live a very uncertain life. Sometimes, it is very hard to see what is really happening to you.

He couldn't control himself on substances, and the trauma buried in his genetics always brought out the worst in him. As a child I never experienced that kind of trauma. I wasn't born into it. There are millions, billions living in abusive relationships worldwide. This is induced into families, communities, cultures and has been for hundreds possibly thousands of years for some regions and peoples of the world. It is perpetuated by the hands of the government institutions, through induced wars, forced displacement, stolen children, broken families, lack of health care, isolation, poverty, homelessness all of which are preventable and unnecessary.

'Be the rock, be strong, a voice, the change you want to see in the world. Hold your belief, trust in your calling, you are loved and cared for. Remember you matter and will always be safe if you do the right thing and uphold your faith.' — Nancy O'Neill AKA 'Is this Justice'

Truly he is my rock and my salvation; he is my fortress, I will not be shaken.
Psalm 62:6

But the Lord is faithful, and he will strengthen you and protect you from the evil one. 2 Thessalonians 3:3

The Lord himself goes before you and will be with you; he will never leave you nor forsake you. Do not be afraid; do not be discouraged. Deuteronomy 31:8

Sometimes there is nothing harder to do than to push forward. Well I did: I left that toxic relationship, and so can you. I moved on to my next journey, one that would prove to bring more pain and suffering, and become a real test of my faith. When your world is turned upside down, what will you do? Will you choose life? I did and continue to endure no matter what my path may be. I know my calling and I choose to keep it in motion. I'm on it! No one can do it for me.

"With great knowledge comes great responsibility." — Haruki Murakami.

My years of living in the Reserves would truly open my eyes, the stories I have been told from elders who attended the Residentials Schools, the Mission Schools, the day homes and the present generations. They talk of the children who were forced to leave their families, hidden sometimes for years and many, their entire lifetime. Some of them were lucky and their parents would hide them from the Indian agents by moving further out into the bush. The suffering caused by the broken families and the loss of their children passes from one generation to the next.

Trauma comes in many forms and you cannot see it in the faces of individuals, but does it ever show in their actions. Mixed with substance abuse, it can become very volatile, devastating, increasing the risk of domestic abuse and others tenfold — all of which could lead to murder, suicide so much unwarranted suffering. It is vital to become aware of your surroundings. Do your research. If you feel you are in a toxic relationship seek out support, try to stay strong, find a counselor, make a shift, a clean break if needed. I was lucky to grow up without verbal or physical abuse but I did live in a home with individuals suffering from mental illness; with a father who functioned with alcoholism. We really don't know the full impacts of trauma in our lives. I thought I had a normal life but now I see it much differently now.

I want people to understand that much trauma is still being imposed on society, cultures, communities, hidden within the institutions and it can be prevented and corrected.

If you wonder why we have so much substance abuse especially for those living within the Reservation, those suffering homelessness, poverty and abuse, it is to mask the generations of trauma. It has truly created a lifetime of struggle for many. It is very difficult for people who have not lived under generations of implied forms of trauma to even understand the impacts. I didn't see things clearly, either — not until massive trauma was applied to our lives. I won't ever forget it.
A person living inside of communities impacted by years of trauma will most likely never have true stability unless the healing happens within. With all the supports in place, it is true healing. Within the Reserves of Canada the impacts are clear to me now after 24 years working and living amongst the people. I want to help them heal. It is a massive task. Hundreds of thousands were impacted by colonization, Residential schools, the 60's Scoop (a movement to replace the Residential Schools as the government continued to remove the (Indian) Indigenous Child from their families in the words of Colonization).

Today the use of Child and Family Services is still committing these unjust activities, totally organized, supported by the Federal Government, and its Institutions, including the Judiciary. Family Law is bringing in millions every year, especially with all related services connected to the illegal apprehensions. I have lived this first hand, defended my family and am still fighting hard to be heard. This is for my family and the 6 First Nation Communities in Northern AB within Treaty 8 Territory and under the governance of Kee Tas Kee Now Tribal Council and Services. I am self taught in various areas of law. Currently I am at the Appeals Court level, I still continue to be met with massive miscarriages of injustices. Yet, I will never stop pushing to be heard until every child, woman, man and person has a voice, I have to start here but it will reach globally. I promise and I always keep my promises!

There are many calls to action on the table, but nothing is being done. I know I continue to be an onlooker for my fellow communities. The forced trauma on my family has opened my eyes to the bigger picture of things. I clearly see that many supports are needed in all services and institutions. Simply saying they are there is not putting them in motion. We need boots on the ground, accessible services relating to health care, education, substance abuse and mental wellbeing. That can only come if we truly do our research in order to help foster the growth of children and families. Society needs a wake up call, a real glimpse into the generations of implied trauma in my community and yours. The impacts are detrimental to how society has developed and the massive suffering we see on a global scale.

Children cannot thrive if they are removed from their families. Families suffer grieving that is never truly addressed. By continuing to share my story, knowledge and teachings, I am doing my part. Never stop learning. Take care of your health at all costs. You cannot help others if you are not well yourself. If you have lived through trauma, share your story and help to empower others. Build a legacy of strength and pride for your children and family. I see oh too clearly that I had to suffer, live a life facing challenges and adversities. It is how I will continue to move forward seeking answers, justice, researching and writing. Trauma is real, and the longer the exposure the more compliance by the impacted victims. We see the implications of the negative impacts of under- and over-diagnosed trauma within society. There must be great awareness brought to what is really molding and shaping the lives of the peoples in my country and yours.

Injustice anywhere is a threat to justice everywhere. — Martin Luther King

"Before we acquire great power we must acquire wisdom to use it well."
— Ralph Waldo Emerson

Any person who has been exposed to traumatic experiences and or Generational Traumas, runs a higher risk of addictions, substance abuse, mischievous behaviors, PTSD, anxiety, depression, stress disorders; the list is extensive. We need to make the proper movements in society and start healing our children, families, communities, nations and the time is now.

"My Beautiful 'Nehiyow' (knee he ow), (to be pure), (the Western Cree), brothers and sisters. When I was a child, I remember saying, "When I grow up, I'm going to marry an Indian," I did. He was very beautiful on the outside and broken within. You cannot see hidden brain trauma on someone's face. It is invisible and comes out in their behaviors and actions." Quote - form A Civil Action 82 pages in length filed April 8th, 2024, by Nancy O'Neill AKA 'Is this Justice'

Within the Residential Schools the children were made to comply or they were heavily abused on multiple levels.Thousands were never returned to their families and within all the residentials schools they had graveyards not playgrounds. The children were sexually, mentally, physiologically abused, and these 'events' changed the very genetics of the people. The impacts continue today and increase with the ease of access to drugs and alcohol within the reservations, compounding the continued implied Generational Trauma over 140 years plus in some regions of Canada.

The people turn to substance abuse which masks the unseen trauma. This imposes more utero exposure (while the baby is in the mother's womb) and much higher rates of substance abuse leading to violence, increased levels of social anxiety, PTSD (Post Traumatic Stress Disorder), suicide and in many cases untimely deaths. We must bring massive awareness to hidden unseen trauma and its impacts on our elderly, youths, those dealing with physical disabilities and or mental illness in society. This is going to be a massive shift in the right direction for all humans. It must be addressed now."

"Most of the important things in the world have been accomplished by people who have kept on trying when there seemed to be no hope at all." —Dale Carnegie

Nancy O'Neill AKA 'Is this Justice,' a mother of five children with Irish, Maliseet and of Cree descent, is an educator, medicinal healer and a peacekeeper. She will continue to devote her life to helping others, becoming a strong advocate for those in need of a voice in her country and soon to be in yours. No stone will be left unturned. Nancy's relentless search for the betterment of humanity keeps her motivated and willing to tackle any unjust, no matter the occurrence. She is the co-author of "Rattled Awake: Volume Eight," an international best-selling book, and a contributor to dozens more anthologies. Ms. O'Neill will continue to seek all opportunities to push forward by learning and applying the law all for the betterment of humanity. Her quest is to reach people globally and make movements for a Utopian future. No one will be left behind.

LinkedIn

Substack

Nancy O'Neill @isthisjustice

"There is a great power in speaking your truth
and standing for something important."

— *Sonita Alizadeh*

REFLECTIONS FROM BRIAN, LEEANNA, JOI & MARK

Brian Luoma
Rattled Awake: Volume Four

After writing my chapter, "Quite The Fish Tail," my fish replica wall art business has taken off. I have since launched a full scale e-commerce website and have been inundated with requests for custom fish pieces from larger agencies and businesses such as interpretive centers, museums and consumers looking for an affordable alternative for realistic fish decor.
https://www.instagram.com/reelisticreplicas/

LeeAna Stock Luoma
Rattled Awake: Volume One

Being one of the authors in the first ever, "Rattled Awake: Volume One" was a little intimidating at first. As a blogger for my own website, dealingwithdiabetes.org, this amazing experience boosted my confidence and enhanced my writing skills. I encourage all of you to take this chance and make your story known. You will be supported by fellow authors, and Lonnee Rey will be with you all the way! LinkedIn

Joi Brooks
Rattled Awake: The Podcasters Edition

Meeting people online is the modern marketplace for professionals and social media has become a virtual break room, filled with Zoom meetings, texts and sound bites. But it's the genuine human connection that ultimately stands out. The gathering of co-authors for Rattled Awake occurred over the span of a single week of my life, but the impact continues. Writing collaborations and opportunities to build connections, like this one, are precious moments in time. emailandcoffee.com

Mark O'Brien, Rattled Awake: The Podcasters Edition. You might come to one of Lonnee's workshops expecting to write about being rattled awake. But the experience of participating will rattle you awake in ways you could never have imagined. If there were a 10-star scoring system around here, I'd give Lonnee and her workshop an 11.
https://dreamvisions7radio.com/the-anxious-voyage/

EMILY SHARRATT...FREEING MOTHER TERESA IN FATIGUES

You become unstoppable when you choose to believe.

Believe in yourself. Believe you are capable. Believe you are lovable.

Believe, see and embrace all of you. Explore, honor, and ask for what you need.

As a former mental health specialist and counselor, I've conferred with enough clients and families to have a professional opinion on this, but in this mini memoir I hope you will indulge me as I confide my own experience with this powerful push and pull phenomenon which rattled me awake and led to the freedom to be myself, receive more, live in both connection and balance.

Yet in order to do this, I would, like so many clients before me, have to suspend my own disbelief in myself in order to make the change.

I would have to recognize, own, feel, sit with, replace, and practice eliminating the thoughts I'd accumulated over a lifetime that were currently keeping me in a space of disconnection and in short, stopping me from reaching the joy, love, and connection I was longing for.

I would have to believe the kind of things others told me. I had to believe the masses, not the minority. I'd have to engineer an environment that would allow me to rebalance and reconnect. And I'd need to find a way to sustain my intentional transformation regardless of setbacks, challenges, and mistakes.

I suspect most of you have had moments in your life when your mind or perception was challenged. Perhaps your struggle was misunderstood? Your story dismissed or discredited? In those moments, we are faced with a choice–although it doesn't often feel that way. It simply feels like the raw stinging smack of an ugly stick. From my counselor chair and personal experiences, I'd often see how the stinging blow is delivered by someone closest to us–someone whose opinion matters to us. And that's easily understood. If the person didn't matter, their words would be easier to forget.

For kids, the words of parents, teachers, and peers become the baseline of the subconscious soundtrack they are shown to start and build their life from. This is why so many professionals emphasize the importance of encouragement to our kids. Telling them all the things they have done right is more powerful in achievement and emotional wellbeing in the short and long run vs. telling them all the things they did wrong and thinking "by being hard on them at home life will feel less hard." That's been proven wrong time and time again by modern psychology as well as evidenced based science and education/child best practices.

As adults, these same soundtracks largely carry forward, but now we add to them the echoes from the world around us. The feedback we hear, so to speak. Depending on how it's delivered to the listener, it can inspire action or it can inspire resistance. Bosses or significant adult relationships, (think of the five people you spend the most time with here), that continue to harp or emphasize your shortcomings usually lead to resentment, burnout, and low motivation to change. If you're the one delivering the message, even if your intent is to help–if you botch the delivery... well, it does really matter what your intent is if I am going to be honest. It's still not a good look if you claim to care about them. You might see a temporary shift, suddenly an employee is on time for three days in a row before falling off the wagon, or your partner puts the dish in the dishwasher–but old patterns return. And with them, resentment of the blunder.

A more powerful intervention to inspire change is using affirmations to reinforce wins through positive psychology. It is much more likely to make change with less collateral damage, to both the relationship between you and the other, as well as the person's sense of competence. And truth be told from what I've observed in my lifetime, making someone feel dumb, does not serve to motivate anyone. It might make you feel good in a moment of frustration, but it will not evoke change.

And if you're about change, and change or improvement matters more to you than being right, this chapter is about to unlock some powerful solutions.

Cognitive Behavioral Psychology is the heavily researched and commonly understood scientific methodology that there is a connection between thought, feeling, and behavior. A thought comes to mind, which leads to a feeling, which leads to a behavior.

You may have heard the term self-talk? This is also a term from this vein of common psychology that's now seen in not just the mental health arena, but mental performance industries, corporate psychology, as well as simple and general social-emotional wellbeing, which is a basic need for all humans. How we speak to others will influence, over time, depending on frequency, duration/closeness of the relationship, how they will begin to speak to themselves in your shared space.

Simplest example I can give–when you have a boss that speaks to you with kindness and respect. Praises you for jobs well done. Acknowledges your contributions and emphasizes their belief in your potential, does it increase your energy and positive feelings or decrease them? Likely increased, from my experience as a leader and manager I've observed these non-tangible people skills increase productivity, retention/wanting to stay at a job, as well as responsibilities/quality of work they bring forth. Oppositely, a boss who speaks poorly to you, tells you all the things you do wrong, does not see where you've gone above and beyond, seems to approach your sense of value and worth with a singularly minded lens is the fast track way to toxic cultures, resentment, poor attendance as well as being someone who has no desire to do their best.

The same is true in how we speak to ourselves.

The words and phrases that shape our realities are the building blocks we use to either build invisible cages we reside to protect ourselves from fear of failure or disappointment, or they are the stairways we build to new solutions, opportunities, and connections.

Where I believe we go wrong is the naivety we have to trust our conscious minds (called 'the ego' in psychology) to be looking for our highest good, and thus telling us the truth in all things. Full stop please. This is Wrong!

Our egos are about keeping us safe. From hurt, from pain, from rejection, from criticism, from ostracizing, etc. Unfortunately, many don't know this basic mechanic of psychology. As a result… they don't question the thoughts that enter their heads. They take them hook, line and sinker. Most especially as they relate to passing judgements upon ourselves and on others. And this is all people, even those of us that have been trained to question our automatic thoughts.

I am a prime example. Let me tell you, for years, my ego did a doozy on me. It felt like falling down an ugly tree and getting smacked by Every. Single. Branch.

Yet, it is because of this knowledge and this culmination of events, my ultimate burnout and disconnection in my personal and professional life, I chose to challenge myself with the questions I would often ask my clients,

What if I listened to my wants and desires… not just listened, but respected, and asked for?

What if I believed, accepted, received the warm, bold, confident observations others graciously gave to me?

What if, instead of dismissing or minimizing their opinion and intelligence to share their kind opinion of me, I honored them? I would certainly take to heart and always turn over negative criticism, why wouldn't I do the same with the generous and kind comments?

And I've seen clients do this hundreds of times. As humans it's something easier to believe in the bad. Less risk of disappointment of falling short that way.

For me, as a result, in order to keep myself small, contained, and a great people pleaser, it was easier to dismiss those kind observations, rather than believing. Or keep them contained to one part of my life, when in another area I may have been acutely aware of my deficits.

But this story of transformation is about Believing. It is about Freedom and it is about Hope. It is about unlocking infinite potential through understanding what is possible when we replace the thoughts that don't serve us with ones that are in connection to our highest good.

As Eleanor Roosevelt so boldly said (and I must agree with her brilliance), "no one can make you feel inferior without your consent."

Over time a thought, be it 50% true, 20% true, or 5% true becomes 100% true when we choose to accept this. For me, I've chosen to believe all kinds of unhelpful or limiting thoughts–for all kinds of reasons. But typically it boils down to safety as humans–either to be loved, be valued, be desired, to be received, to be worthy/enough, etc.

Long ago in graduate school, due to my training in Trauma Response with Women and Children, I learned that living in connection is a powerful avenue to evoke healing, happiness, and hope. Conversely, living in disconnection has been scientifically shown to exacerbate, prolong, and create additional psychological suffering. That suffering feels one way to the individual, but oftentimes it comes out as irritability, aggression, defensiveness, sadness, difficulty thinking clearly, withdrawing, changes in memory, increased feelings of isolation or loneliness, anger or resentment, and the loss of feeling competent. Can you relate to any of these feelings?

When you look back at those moments in your life, what was going on? Do you feel you were connected to yourself or disconnected? What about the others around you?

Living in connection, once we're here, feels like soaring confidence, acceptance, feeling balanced and grounded, we speak kindly to ourselves and honor others, and our ability to give and receive love. Closely related emotions like joy, become intuitive and easy. The resistance to feeling in this state evaporates because we are no longer in a state of numbness, survival mode, or a suspended state of denial to our highest good. We have drawn boundaries and in short have created an environment where we can thrive. We are no longer a fish in a tree, but a fish in the water.

When we are living in disconnection we feel easily winded, our energy fluctuates too frequently, our perceptions of emotional wellbeing and physical wellbeing become exacerbated.

For me, these are examples of the limiting thoughts I personally adopted by 2022…ones that led to my feeling of disconnection. In essence, they were the invisible bars my ego mind had told me over time, hearing them from others or a similar vein, and I'd believe them. I'd literally built a cage of my own making, put myself in it, and thought it had been out of my own highest good.

As you read my authentic thoughts below, please also notice the action that associates with the thought. That is the power of Cognitive Behavioral Science. There is a factual truth that what we think, thus feel, absolutely drives how we act.

"I am mean" – thus I compensated by not speaking, hoping my sacrifice of voice will allow others comfort. Hurting others in my effort to love warmly, unconditionally, and respectfully would be the opposite of my desire to heal/bring relief and joy to others. So I shrink and become a ghost, just floating through the motions but not fully participating.

"I am hard to love" – thus I feel guilty for asking what I need, so I stop asking. In the meantime, my heart atrophies and I recede onto myself. My light dims and capacities to do what I am intrinsically designed to do: Connect. I worry I am a burden to be in connection with, so I shrink myself for fear I am 'too much' or that I am 'only of value as the nurturer of others, not to receive for myself.'

"I am crazy" – I began to doubt my emotional fortitude and strength, as opposed to allowing the scientist in me to acknowledge what this really was. It was not psychosis, loss of judgment, or lack of competence–it was a trauma response after too much vicarious trauma and an environment that could not sustain balance for me.

As a person who feels my greatest gift is my ability to love, receive love, and show others how to love, you can see how these prominent and destructive thoughts would be the bars on a very effective prison I built. That as a result it was I that kept myself in disconnection.

At the same time, the truth and hope within that is I could get myself out.

The work that would go into overturning and reframing these thoughts would take time and effort, but I knew it would be worth it. Now standing two years out, I can say, IT IS!!

1) I needed to design the right environment for myself as a fish who is expected to fly like a bird, will go its whole life thinking itself incapable, unlovable, or unworthy of connection. I needed to create a space I could heal.

   a) I would need to step away from a job that I loved, but could no longer emotionally sustain. I was crying every morning on my way to work, scared for the safety situations that I could no longer truly protect. One of my students had been committed of murder and my heart deeply ached for them, but the reality that I was not Mother Teresa in Fatigues–I could not protect, save, and care for all, left me in an existential crisis.

b) I would need to change my family structure as much as it pained both of us to do so. I would then also need to withdraw from social media. Learn to live alone for the first time in my life. And learn how to be the best single parent I could possibly be. This was by far the hardest thing to do. And I am tremendously grateful for the child-aligned and respectful co-parenting relationship I share with an intelligent man who is a great father.

2) I would need to allow myself to feel. To stop being numb. I'd need to feel in order to be motivated to act and start the process to move from disconnection to connection.

a) This meant no more stuffing of feelings. No more being stoic as that's what a Mother Teresa in Fatigues is expected to do. I was able to move off my antidepressants after physically changing environments as well as to quit smoking which I'd picked up during Covid due to the isolation. The chemical escape was something that had made the general disconnection I felt within myself tolerable. No longer needing either, when it was the right time, were incredible wins for me personally.

b) I had to accept I could not change anyone. This was very hard for me as I was a counselor, a very good one– I'd been the youngest member elected onto the state advisory council for the Department of Elementary and Secondary Education to guide best practice across the state as well as to reinforce suicide prevention– I'd been trained in all kinds of counseling modalities in terms of what to say/how to say it to elicit change "change talk." These ultimately are seeds to change we might instill in others to lead to healing, growth, or development that could alleviate hardship for the individual. Yet, in reality, even with this knowledge I could not change individuals that were not my clients. They did not want it, nor was that my role. And if the lack of change was causing suffering in me that I did not have the power to shield from, I'd need to redefine my space. For me, I'd need to learn boundaries–but not self-sabotage myself through guilt by believing "I am mean" for having boundaries or limitations.

3) And the hardest thing: I would need to act. By disassembling a life that was safe, familiar, yet simultaneously leading me to burnout and ruin.

a) This meant leaving the clients whom I loved, but no longer felt strong enough to help. Losing touch with my colleagues and a community 40 minutes from my home I'd cared for over a decade was excruciating, especially in the years to follow.

b) I would yes to a corporate job that promised more balance, and financial means to bring safety and security to my life.

c) The hardest though was moving through a divorce after 12 long years with someone who helped me for many years and whom we shared a beautiful son together. And then to live alone for the first time in my life at 36 years old while grieving and growing wellness at the same time.

But I will be honest: I did none of this alone.

As alone as I may have felt. I was never alone. Because that is the beauty of opening yourself up to connection. Once you forgo the stoic drum chant of hyper independence our society holds as the gold standard, it becomes easier to be thoughtful with vulnerability, intentional, and successfully acknowledge moments of connection.

I feel that this emphasis of hyper independence is important to mention as members of a society (USA) that puts on pillars those who embody complete independence and often will minimize or dismiss individual achievements that were the result of accepting help from others, be it emotional, psychical, or financial. It somehow makes them view themselves as less gritty or incredible for making huge lifestyle changes in very hard times. As a counselor I would often notice clients felt ashamed to accept support from people in their lives. There seemed to be guilt to receive this help and as a result it would paralyze people from acting, the perceived shame or guilt only leading to longer suffering instead of faster healing. At the same time, I get the need to want to do it ourselves.

As I said, I used to be Mother Teresa in Fatigues. She doesn't ask for Help, she *is* the Help.

Back to what I alluded to above. The work. How did I do it, make the change? And how amazing is this change? How worthwhile is it to be in connection? Such great questions, you ask!!

I used a variety of techniques on myself to begin to break down these unhelpful building blocks of my inner judgements and replaced them with new ones.

Life the first year after divorce was a wrecking ball of thoughts, feelings, and emotions—for those of you who can relate, do you remember? For anyone who's been through a significant life event and rallied from the ashes, I imagine you can also relate. Our minds become a regular demolition zone and reconstruction site.

I started with a Western style psychology approach within Cognitive Behavioral Science. You single out the thoughts that are most limiting to you and simply put, not true. You find examples of how it is not true. You think on those points. Have conversations on those points with yourself or a friend. For me, I liked to journal.

I had to remind myself that I was capable and lovable.

I selected a thought replacement strategy I'd done with countless clients over the years, individually, even professional to professional on a building, community and state level, but really it's simply lending a person a compliment, only the compliment is just above where the person (or this case me) feel we are truly at. In order for it to work best, eye contact should be made. It creates a highway for the words to better take root. If you use it with a partner, child, employee, or colleague look them in the eye while saying it. If it's just you, look yourself in the mirror as you say it and hold eye contact. If you pull away your gaze, break eye contact, dismiss the statement, or can't get through saying the statement for yourself– that's your clue right there you are resisting it and don't want to believe, more than your ego wants to keep you 'safe and small' (by allowing you to think something less than that thought.) My simple advice is to keep at it. Everyday reread your replacement thought, memorize it, stare yourself in the eyes and don't let up until you can look into your eyes and intuitively feel the connection.

I wrote with a dry erase marker; I've most often seen individuals use post-it notes; but the first three affirmations I started with to replace the negative tape-recorder I'd been permitting to live in my mind had to go.

I wrote, "I am Lovable."
(Sometimes I'd switch it to, "I am easy to love.")

"I am capable."

"A balanced life full of joy is on its way."

As a woman with ADHD my natural cadence is different and as a result different can be seen as difficult by the outside world. As my intent was not to be 'difficult,' we go about trying to get our needs met in a world not built for us, oftentimes frustrating or confusing (example sarcasm is so hard for me as I am very literal, hence my writing style, almost academic, right?) Straightforward, efficient. Neurodivergent folks generally deeply appreciate efficiency, predictability, and the ability to anticipate. Although we are spontaneous and love to dive down rabbit holes of new thoughts, ideas. We generate innovation and curiosity in the right setting. Many of us might have a gift for predicting outcomes. I myself have found this to be true as I've been tested by a neurology department as I was so worried my memory was 'so bad' because it felt so far from my other skills and so difficult for me I felt it must be a deficit, or I must be 'crazy.' Surprise, surprise, the Neurologist and Psychologist team determined my memory is within the normal range, it just feels like a deficit because I am gifted in two other areas. My memory requires more cognitive labor on my part so the struggle in and of itself makes me 'feel' it's a deficit, at the same time trauma and stress for anyone can exacerbate memory struggles for anyone. But as I said above, when you're a fish, who's expected to be a bird, you can go your whole life thinking you're less than the gift you are.

Two years ago it took me three months to get through those positive affirmations without any resistance. When I first started, I could not read them without looking away and crying, shaking my head and angrily saying out loud, "I can't do this". That's how hard this work is for those that truly have the courage to transform. But after three months of daily reciting, I was able to look in the mirror with a smile, and grin saying with confidence, certainty, and conviction: "I AM easy to LOVE", "I AM CAPABLE", and "BALANCED LIFE full of JOY is coming." And this was a springboard into stronger and stronger affirmations since that time, each becoming a force multiplier to all areas of my life–be it personal or professional.

In addition to the Self-Talk Replacement Affirmation, I practiced a wonderful new age science methodology my mother, also a Social Worker at Speaker, taught me starting around the age of nine years old. It's through the HeartMath Institution and the technique is designed to create alignment between your mind and heart. Some call it a state of 'flow' or being in 'the zone,' but HeartMath calls it Heart Coherence. To achieve this heart-mind connection (which really is simply calming my Fight, Flight or Freeze response) by inducing feelings of gratitude and self-compassion while deep breathing and thus increasing joy and a feeling alert calm competence. Doing this for 5-20 minutes a day, several times a week, really started to speed up feeling like myself again.

My final favorite strategy I used is an ancient Hawaiian forgiveness technique and self-healing practice called HoOponopono. As someone trained in Trauma Response from a scientific evidence-based lens, I was blown away at the instant relief I started to feel from using this technique. It felt like the power of receiving multiple therapy sessions combined into a short and powerful burst of emotional relief, and instead of costing me thousands, it was Free99. I could hardly believe it. I teach this technique to clients now as it is an absolute game-changer. All it took was some courage and vulnerability on my side to do something different. In simple explanation, HoOponopono is a self-love technique which involves four components: I am sorry, please forgive me, I am sorry, I love you. It's a strong tool for anyone's toolbox to transmute especially stubborn and resistant thoughts you can't seem to shake, thus opening yourself up to receive the replacement thoughts you're working with daily on a conscious level in front of the mirror.

Since starting this transformation, striving to live in connection instead of disconnection from myself, I have found balance, joy, and tremendous opportunity in my professional and personal life. I have rebuilt a life I feel deeply connected to simply by suspending my disbelief that the invisible bars of self-deprecating thoughts were for my highest good and have done the consistent and relief bringing work to replace those thoughts with those that are in closer alignment.

And surprise, surprise, incredible things have happened and are now happening faster and faster, especially as I grow the power of my affirmations to those that are more complex or abundant. I have said yes, and am continuing to be in awe of saying 'yes' to more opportunities for Joy, while continuing to help individuals, partners, families, teams, and communities to transform and reach their next level wellness. I write and publish books that inspire and teach, two which are co-authored international bestsellers. As a result, I am being invited into places where my messages can evoke and empower audiences with speaking as well as writing and coaching. Big projects are manifesting without stress and resistance because I've gotten out of my own way. This fall, my first solo publication, in 2022, *Rainbow Brain: Mindset Matters*, will debut in a second edition, this time ripe with illustrations by an Internationally Bestselling illustrator in South Africa. The book's message of positive self-talk in relation to a growth mindset and self-love will even get air time in front of a television audience of 52 million! What a milestone and dream reached. The television station will even be promoting a Wellness Retreat Weekend in the New Year I've been requested to lead with three others. I don't feel stretched thin, overworked, helpless to do more, or guilty for time away from my son as I work around his and my schedule. In the meantime, I am a great mom, friend, daughter, and force multiplier to those who come into my orbit. Life has gotten better since I've done the mindset work, and I hope my courage to be transparent with you, both professionally, and personally will also motivate you to seek deeper connection within yourself, your relationships and the larger world.

I'd be honored to help support or lead your next Wellness Day at work or in the community, please reach out to me on LinkedIn. As an individual drawn to my message, I'd be honored to contribute to the deeper connections you foster within your own life. Reach out on LinkedIn for coaching packages either for group work or one on one. I have a Podcast coming soon, but am always drawn as a light to help those that dare ask for it–because I promise, you and what you believe to be your singular issue, is not just yours. It's amazing the overlap we share and by helping one, we help more.

Emily Sharratt, MSW, is on a mission to increase the joy and wellbeing we experience as individuals within our relationships, teams, & communities. She brings unique experience as a former Master level Social Worker and High School Counselor, as well as neurodivergent businesswoman and mother. As an award-winning author, speaker, and leader, Emily champions the transformative power of gratitude and compassion, not just for others, but for ourselves, to stay better not bitter through life's storms and sunny skies. She's the Author of *Rainbow Brain: Mindset Matters* and 2x Rattled Awake Co-Author, Vol. 9, The Writers & Poets Edition, and Vol. 10, "The Liberty Issue."

REFLECTIONS FROM EMILY

Emily Sharratt
Rattled Awake: Vol 9, "The Writers & Poets Edition"

 Since my first publication in Volume 9, my opportunities have skyrocketed— invitation for TV airtime in front of an audience of 52 Million, leading an incredible Wellness Weekend Retreat in Chicago, + elevating my first solo publication to help our next generation springboard into confidence and joy.

The writing experience helped not only by brand and confidence as a coach, trainer and speaker, but also as a woman—healing through connection with both my writing, the process, and the people involved.

Lonnee Rey brings clarity in the chaos that often keeps writers paralyzed and stuck, unable to share our greatest gift, our story, with those that most need to hear it. I can't recommend enough contributing your voice to the Rattled Awake best selling series.

REFLECTIONS FROM PETER

Peter J. Merrick
Rattled Awake: Volumes 8, 9 & 10

Having the honor to participate in three volumes of the Rattled Awake book series has been a rewarding professional journey. The key highlight has been my collaboration with Lonnee Rey, the visionary behind  the series. As a skilled book producer, award-winning editor, ghostwriter, and story development coach, Lonnee provides invaluable insights and tips that have significantly enhanced my work. Her dedication to self-publishing is truly inspiring.

Our professional relationship has broadened my perspective on writing and business, pushing me to new heights and encouraging deeper, more authentic expression. This experience has been pivotal for my growth and creative evolution.

Peter J. Merrick - PeterMerrick.com

PETER J. MERRICK...TAKING THINGS AWAY UNTIL ONE SAYS YES IS NOT A CHOICE!

I wish I could introduce you to Larry – if you knew him you would love him. By knowing Larry, you immediately understood why he owned every room he ever entered. He was the unofficial mayor of every community he became a part of.

But Larry has been gone for three years now. Let Larry's story and death be the call to action – the catalyst to speak your truths from the top of your lungs. It has become mine and this short chapter is me yelling from the rooftops that we are in the worst trouble of all. A truth that should never be silenced to wrong doings.

On this 4th of July 2024, this is a Canadian Expat writing on a Canadian story which is truly a universal story that we all need to share. As Ronald Reagan once famously warned us in a speech he gave on March 30, 1961:

"Freedom is never more than one generation away from extinction. We didn't pass it to our children in the bloodstream. It must be fought for, protected, and handed on for them to do the same."

Reagan forewarned all the people of the world that freedom is always at risk and can vanish within a generation if not defended. It's not automatically passed down; each generation must fiercely protect and fight for it to ensure its survival for the next, or risk losing it forever. And this is why the story of Larry Liepic, a proud Canadian must be told. We must learn and we must speak up against tyranny when it comes at us.

To be silenced is to allow yourself to become a slave. This is worse than death itself - to be a slave to an immoral system, run by those that are allowed to rule unjustly, illegally, sadistically, and satanically over us.

I wish I could pick up the phone right now to call Larry - to tell him about my day. I hope this tribute to my friend will begin my personal healing process and give honor to a life cut unnecessarily too short.

Since the Call - I have walked about my days in San Diego - thinking back to my old life and what I loved most about living in Toronto. Now - I find myself muttering – I miss my BIG SOUL BROTHER – Larry. In my world he was one of those unique individuals that made my memory of Toronto – MEMORABLE - HOME!

How best to describe him - who was Larry Lipiec? This is the question I keep asking myself. In my world Larry was bigger than life. My journey was made much richer because of his kindness, wit, smarts, wisdom, charm, friendship, and love.

I can still hear our laughter. Just thinking of Larry makes me smile. As I type this sentence, I can still see his big grin in my head. He was in the plus column for all who were privileged to call him friend.

Larry was so special in that way. He just made life bigger, funnier, better, and livelier. He had the most infectious smile. No one had a better sense of humor – whatever your situation Larry had the unique gift to give you a new perspective while making your ribs hurt from laughter. There was a way and wisdom about him that made life less serious and more light.

It feels just like yesterday when we first met – it was the night of Halloween 2001 – in the weeks following 9/11. Looking back- those events were the starting point of our democracies' dark descent into night – into totalitarianism. I remember after our first conversation that evening being filled with soulful laughter; I left saying to myself – I really like this guy.

Everyone Loved Larry. Imagine the deep connection you have to a brother. He had that enchanting charm about him. He made everyone feel like they were family - that you were special – that your life counted. He was always open to lending a helping hand and sharing his ear, giving guidance to those who were smart enough to ask for it.

Our meeting was synchronistic - he was a practicing Wills and Estate Lawyer. I was in need of his services to complement my financial planning business. Back then I was an active Certified Financial Planner with dozens of clients that needed their wills completed. My clients all loved being introduced to Larry – how could they not. Over two decades later I am still asked how is your good friend Larry – saying: "I really liked him – he was funny, professional, charming, thorough, and a very memorable character."

Yes - he was a BIGGER than life character! Larry was one of the most gifted communicators I had ever witnessed in action. Live audiences, radio listeners, television viewers and commentators would almost wet their pants listening to him sharing his endless stories, observations, jokes, and anecdotes.

I remember one evening watching Larry sell hundreds of his do-it yourself Will Kits on the Home Shopping Cable Channel. I fell off my seat laughing when a mother called into the live show asking if they could set him up with her daughter. That was Larry – peculiar things always came his way.

At the dawn of the new millennium - Larry had been recently divorced, and boy could he make you laugh about the lessons and bruises he learned from it firsthand. Only Larry could get away and carry off his next project with his flair for theatrics and dry sense of humor. He wrote a bestselling book titled - I Had Dreams of a Happy House - Now I'm a Former Spouse. In it he shared his misadventures of navigating dating, marriage, divorce, parenting, the legal system, and how to survive to the other side.

Larry was a fun, harmless, loveable, playful neurotic – he owned this title with pride. Even though he was the most extraordinary salesman and marketer you would ever meet, unfortunately, this was not enough. He needed his patterns and security requirements met. You could set your clock by Larry's schedule. This anxiety eventually took hold of him. It prevented him and the world from fully realizing his true potential and enjoying in his innate charms.

In late 2003 – Larry decided to go back to Transport Canada as a prosecuting attorney where he had worked for the first decade after he had graduated from law school. Boy did he love the thoughts of future security and the comforts of a government job – the ability to pilot airplanes and that damned guaranteed government pension that he so looked forward to and relished having in retirement.

Larry had so much to look forward to. He had lots of friends and family that adored him, a large government pension, plenty of savings in the bank and a pending magistrate judgeship appointment after he retired. The COVID lunacy and the tyrants administrating this tyranny took away all that he had to look forward towards.

Larry was a proud Canadian and he believed in Canada – a country founded on the rule of law, its 1982 Constitution and its Charter of Rights and Freedoms. This is why he watched in horror as the governments of Canada broke the social contract, they had with each of its citizens – quickly stripping away his and his fellow Canadians rights of having complete autonomy over their own bodies, their health care choices, their privacy, the rights to movement, the right for the freedom of association, the right of freedom of speech and to be treated equally under the law.

Larry was not an anti-jabber – he had every shot known to man before this last one. He was the epitome of health. He was also a lawyer and a damn good one at that. Through his training and experience he read every word in every label and every contract to comprehend what he was getting himself into. He had decided that no one was going to force him to sign onto an experimental medical procedure without his informed consent.

An experimental medical procedure that had not been proven to work or to be safe.

Larry would share that he believed that these morally bankrupt elected representatives, unelected bureaucrats, corporate and non-governmental organizational gangsters lie to us each day telling us that their motives behind their mandates were pure and their punishments were in our best interests.

Larry was a cautious individual, he liked easing into his change. But because of all the illegal mandates stripping him of his human rights, he felt forced into making some quick dramatic life changes to secure his personal freedoms. If the events of the Covid years had not been thrust upon him, he would have eased slowly into his transition, and we would still have my friend with us today.

He was a workaholic – having banked 85 days of vacation pay and 30 days of sick leave he was going to take a long vacation permanently to Mexico to retire. This would allow him to avoid being put on administrative leave without pay because he chose to rightfully keep his medical information private from his employer – The Government of Canada.

Larry booked a first-class one-way ticket to Acapulco for October 28, 2021 – one day before the mandates were to be enforced denying all Canadians the right to fly on planes if they did not have their Jab Papers in order.

The day Larry arrived in Mexico he received a courtesy call from Ontario Health – the Ontario Province Administrator of its single payer socialistic medical plan to tell him that he had not gotten his shot and they would gladly arrange his appointment to get his. He did not know what made him more upset – the fact that his medical privacy had been breached unlawfully by his government or that call had originated from an outsourced call center contracted in Pakistan.

I was so proud of Larry for making such a big move – taking hold of his destiny. We spoke regularly for the first few weeks while he was in Acapulco. I had planned to visit him for a few weeks to explore Mexico and to give him some familiarity of home as he adjusted.

I was hard on Larry during some of our phone conversations when he would sometimes say in passing that he was thinking about going back to Canada. Being a Canadian in Exile and living with the thought of never seeing his native home again made him very upset, anxious, and sad. Towards the end of his stay, I received this text that summed up how he was feeling living away from home in self-imposed exile:

I am better today. Let me just think Peter. I really thank you for what you said yesterday. 62 years of conditioning has F**KED me up. When I put my mind to anything I can do it.

Larry often stated that he knew what awaited him if he returned to Canada. To him the Canada he had once loved had fallen to full blown totalitarianism. Upon his return he would be locked away in his home under house arrest - not allowed to participate in regular society – having his basic human rights stripped away and denied him.

All orchestrated by the Tyrannical Mechanical Anti-Human Regime that had whipped-up Canadians into Mass Hysteria – into fearing normal contact with one's own neighbors, their family, and fellow Canadians. All this discrimination sanctioned by a tyrannical government that aimed to discriminate against its citizens that legally chose to exercise their guaranteed Canadian Constitutional Rights to say NO!

It had been a few days since I had last heard from Larry. I was beginning to become worried. By this time in his stay in Mexico he was only communicating through text. In one of my last texts to him I sent this JPG to celebrate his transition into his new stage of life:

After that text I did not hear back from Larry for a few days. The change he had embarked on six weeks earlier had been too much for him to handle. His last text to me was sent on December 12, 2021, and it read:

This is your reminder that if you still have not caved to the powers that be, you've just survived the greatest psyop in human history, a plan that has been in the works for decades.

Do you realize how much time, resources, money & effort they put into this? They studied every possilble way to manipulate, brainwash and coerce you. They tried to demoralize you by corrupting society from every possible corner. They tried to vilify you, desensitize you, scare you, guilty you and shame you. They tried to lure you with money, gifts and rewards. They tried to confuse you and make you question your reality and even your sanity at times. They tried to get you to abandon your own principles, values, morals and ethics. They even turned those close to you against you.

Almost everyone fell for it. But not you. So just sit back for a moment and realize how much you've weathered over these past 20 months. Yet you never gave in! You stood your ground against all odds. And not only did you not drop to your knees, you rose like a Phoenix in the night and stepped fully and completely into your power.

WELL DONE

Hi Peter,

I came back to Canada. Please don't be mad at me. Please don't call me now. I have to sleep. I have to keep my phone on because the government calls regularly to check in on me. To make sure I stay locked-down and locked-in my home. When I am up to it, I will call you. I am very down. I just hope I can

continue living like this. I love you. It was my decision to come back and I have to live with it. I felt too vulnerable and was scared if I got sick there, I would be all alone. I was not having a good time there because I was so anxious.
Larry

That was the last time I heard from Larry. I tried multiple times to reach out to him but there was no response. Then two weeks later I got the dreaded call. Larry was found dead at his home in Toronto on Sunday, December 26, 2021.

Now - Larry is dead – there is no pension - there is no security – there is no retirement - there is no doubt in my mind - Larry was a casualty to this tyranny brought onto all of us - commencing March 2020. No one can silence me nor will convince me in believing otherwise.

One of Larry's last wishes was to have his ashes spread over the Pacific Ocean. This has not yet happened, but I hope to be there when this wish is granted. There was a memorial service for him a few days before the end of 2021 at his home in Toronto. I felt fortunate to watch on a cell camera as so many people celebrated Larry's life.

There are two types of individuals we meet as we walk this earth: givers and takers. Larry for so many was a life giver. Not just to me but also to countless others. Since Larry's passing, I have listened to story after story about how much he had touched their lives - individuals from all walks of life in positive, important, meaningful and magical ways.

One individual life may not seem that important in the big scheme of things. What is important is the meaning that we draw from witnessing that life lived. I am so proud to have witnessed and been a part of Larry Lipiec's life and him being on my journey as well.

I am not upset at Larry for leaving us much too soon. However, I am plenty mad at those that brought us into this current dystopian era and the overwhelming number of sheeple that have acquiesced to tyranny, evil and tyrants.

ON THIS JULY 4TH AS WE CELEBRATE THE INDEPENDENCE OF THE UNITED STATES - We MIGHT NOT HAVE LARRY. FOR ME HE WAS NOT JUST ANOTHER NAMELESS CASUALTY TO THIS STUPIDITY AND TYRANNY THAT WE ALL HAVE SUFFERED FROM DURING THIS WORLDWIDE HOAX PERPETRATED BY CRIMINALS ON THE ENTIRETY OF HUMANITY!

BUT I WILL REMEMBER, I WILL SPEAK UP, I WILL NOT BEND THE KNEE TO TYRANNY. I INVITE YOU TO STAY VIGILANT AND FIGHT FOR EVERY FREEDOM AND LIBERTY UNTIL YOUR LAST BREATH. THIS IS HOW WE HONOR LARRY AND OTHERS WE HAVE LOVED THAT HAVE FALLEN.

ON THIS JULY 4TH, 2024 REMEMBER THE WORDS OF PRESIDENT RONALD REAGAN:

"Freedom is never more than one generation away from extinction. We didn't pass it to our children in the bloodstream. It must be fought for, protected, and handed on for them to do the same."

Peter J. Merrick is proud to have participated in three volumes of "Rattled Awake." He loves writing and wakes up at 5:30 AM each morning to write for two hours on topics that catch his attention. He is a Trust and Estate Practitioner (TEP) with the Society of Trust and Estate Practitioners (STEP), the largest global professional body of cross-disciplinary professionals focusing on international planning for multi-generational families. Peter's career in cross-border risk management, business succession consulting, financial education, and writing has been extensive since the early 1990s. He seeks simple solutions to complex financial, tax, and estate planning problems. Peter has authored three comprehensive LexisNexis textbooks on Business Succession Planning and Estate Planning and published over 800 articles. His work has appeared in Bloomberg, The Wall Street Journal, Dow Jones, and numerous other magazines, professional trade papers, and journals. A Canadian Expat residing in San Diego, California, and a Citizen of the World, Peter specializes in cross-border and risk management for US non-American nationals, business owners, professionals, their families, and trusted advisors. He identifies wealth-saving opportunities in cross-border US and international planning using US Life Insurance and Annuity strategies. Peter can be reached at 858.264.9595 or 416.854.1776, or via email at peter@petermerrick.com and PeterMerrick.com.

LONNEE REY...REFLECTIONS
ON THE BACK NINE

We don't receive wisdom; we must discover it
for ourselves after a journey that no one can
take for us, or spare us. -Marcel Proust

How true...however, this is also true:

*"It's important to learn from your mistakes, but it is
BETTER to learn from other people's mistakes, and
it is BEST to learn from other people's successes.
It accelerates your own success."* — *Jim Rohn*

There is no greater agony than bearing an
untold story inside you. -Maya Angelou

Definitely. But let's set aside the notion that you have to rip off a scab and share it publicly to have a meaningful story and impact. (Please see a diverse range of Rattled Awake topics I have covered in editions 1-9, below.)

Reaching more people also equates to more than just a solid message or news they can use: it means doing it faster. A quickie. (Where did *your* mind just go?) JK

"Short reads" are wildly popular for a reason. MINI-memoirs are, too.

Taking a chapter out of your life IS a mini-memoir, dear reader. You might be "Rattled Awake" to know that -?

The AHA you had could be the very thing that alters the path for others. Sharing is caring. Don't underestimate the value of your personal journey.

Memoirs, like chapter books, carry a message for the readers. Work with someone who sees you from the outside, often seeing more than you can for yourself. This is what a story development editor does: they see the big picture, down the road and around the corner, *for* you. The 'write' person can help you craft your message.

The worst advice ever: you need 50k words and 10 chapters to have a "real" book. "Finish rates" drop drastically at 100+ pages (from 60% to 25%.) Please, before you write/overwrite, consider these truths:

Don't go all the way just yet...

"Longer" is not always better.
(Slim & short
is where its at.)

"All night long"
is far too long.

"Knocking one out" isn't so hard,
after all.

Let passion be your guide.

Do it with others...

It's more fun than just one.

Find a space and a place
where all words are "safe."

Sure, it gets messy sometimes...

(comes with the territory.)

AND, THERE IS ALWAYS
A HAPPY ENDING

I have been rattled by the events of our days almost

everyday. There is so much going on it can be overwhelming, I know. What can we do about it?

We must enhance the light, not fight
the darkness. -A. D. Gordon

Action alleviates anxiety. If something is on your mind, it is still in your heart. Dear One, please do the thing that calls to you.

The world is changed by your example,
not by your opinion. -Paulo Coelho

These are my Rattled Awake stories since the series began in August, 2023. As you will see, there are both informative as well as transformative events, all written with you in mind:

Self-effacing humor is a great way to deliver information. , as you will see in this honest account of facing my worst fear: a pressure canner.

I was more afraid of that pressure canner than public speaking. This is the story of what happens when your 'why?' overcomes your 'hell no.'

"The Pressure Cooker" -read by Author Lonnee Rey

"It all started when I ran into some alarming headlines on alternative news platforms. The terrible decimation of crops that are not going to come back, and the loss of nearly two thousand food processing plants, coincidentally all due to fire, led to my permanently raised eyebrow. What the heck was going on?? As far as food went, the writing was on the wall. It wasn't just some crazy preppers being hoarders of food for a pending Armageddon. This was real and it was happening right under our noses. The bigger alarm was that few people knew about this. With all the crazy things happening in our world, I wanted to make sure that at least one thing in my life would be secure.

I like to eat. I'm thinking, *it's a good idea.* I'm really not trying to fast. I know they recommend it, but I'm not really trying to do that right now, or in the future. The news I read was disturbing enough. It's hard to do anything when we are not at peace. What's also true is

that we can think better when we're not hungry. We hear about inflation or other things like that lately. All of these things want to steal our peace. **If you know it's going to rain, grab an umbrella**."
Rattled Awake: Volume One - Kindle

"THIS BUGS ME"

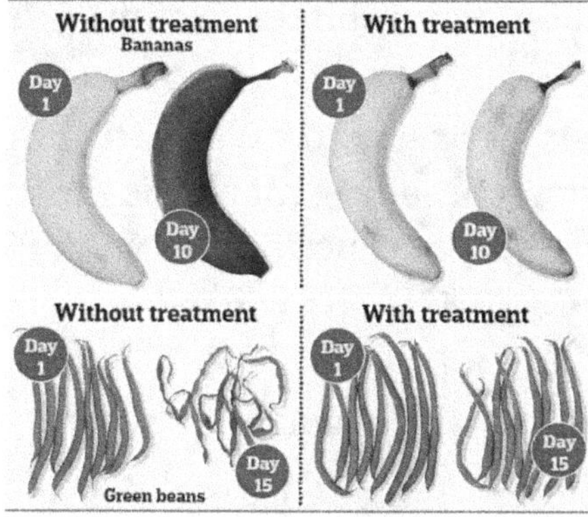

Read by the author,
Rattled Awake:
Volume Two
Lonnee Rey

Bugs Are for Bait. Not for the plate!
This Bugs Me - read by the author

"...and then there is the magnetic meat. What's that - you say you didn't see it on the news? Cue shock face. Tell-lie-vision - if you only get half the truth, what's the other half?

If you want to know more of what the real news is today, I have intentionally posted multiple platforms as reference links (in this chapter.) I spent years discerning the shills from the sages. Do your own research and stay abreast of changes in our food supply and policics that will impact you or your kids. They are already encouraging kids to eat bugs at some US schools. Yeah, no kidding.

Back to the magnetic meat. I'll let this video do ALL the talking. A rattled awake moment here was that the name brand, Simple Truth Organics, also tested positive for magnetism. I was like, Damn there goes another one."

Jan 31, 2022 MAGNETIC MEAT - TIM TRUTH
https://www.bitchute.com/video/K8YDlwACBfa6/

This guy revisited Walmart in August 2023 to see if they were still selling magnetic meat. #SHORT
https://youtube.com/shorts/oP3LTkPpMwU?
si=LgqtQOOstNKwSDV2

GET Rattled Awake: Volume Two Volume Two - Kindle edition

"Pippi Longstocking" stories inspired me as a kid; being divinely-guided, following "The BIG Yes!", led the way. Hilarious misadventures and manifesting magic that will inspire you to trust life, and yourself, are within these pages:

The Art of Traveling Light - Read by Author Lonnee Rey

"The Mississippi trip was a BIG Yes! I never told Dad how our kayak was overtaken and nearly-sunk by tugboat waves in the first hour down river. Why would I? He'd only worry…

Dave was hosting "Yestival" in the fall of that year. They named the main stage The BIG Yes Tent. I was floored, honored and rightfully flattered. A couple years later, I was a speaker to 400 adventurers. What an incredible experience – all because I got a feeling I should go hear this skateboard dude's talk (while living in Australia.)

But wait, there's more: We visited a blues club after the river trip ended. Lucky timing: BB King, Jr., was on stage in a pop-up show. It'd been 25 years since he played there. We hit it off. In fact, I ended-up being his manager, and also throwing him a 74th birthday party in Charleston, SC. See what happens when you follow your BIG Yes?"
Rattled Awake: Volume Three

What do you do when you discover your family has been lying to you about so many things? One of those lies, a half-sister who supposedly died at birth, became evident recently when she showed-up in a Facebookmessage. How do you recover? This, and a few other 'gems' are discussed in:

Untying the Knots - Read by Author Lonnee Rey

"If you have ever wondered WTF, why do I stop short, what's this guilt I'm carrying, (maybe it ain't all childhood trauma), or, when is it going to be MY turn?!?!, you are not alone. If this chapter does nothing else but point you to a possible resolution, then typing this puppy with one finger, all 3,448 words and 10 hours invested, was totally worth it.

Wherever you have raised yourself up out of, whatever it took for you to get this far, bless you! You, too, have lived to tell about. Please share your rattled awake story and become a story-healer. Your message matters more than you realize." Rattled Awake: Volume Four - Kindle

A 10-alarm fire rattled us all awake. The survivors were starting life over the way it began: barefoot, in pajamas, shivering cold and wondering, NOW WHAT? It inspired me to show you how to prepare in case of an evacuation:

COULD YOU GET OUT IN 3 MINUTES - or less?

Peace of Mind

**Read by the author,
Rattled Awake: Volume
Five
Lonnee Rey**

Peace of Mind - read by author Lonnee Rey

"Think of it as 'camping, light.' Start by making a list of what you have, or will need, to address the four main aspects: shelter, fire, food, first-aid. Dedicate three hours on a Saturday to build your 'exit, stage right' bag. Dedicate two hours to assemble vital documents and also load them onto a USB memory stick. If you bought new shoes, dedicate time to breaking them, now. You may want to spray them, as well as your chosen jacket/coat, with water repellant.

If you have a family, you can split-up the heavier items between the adults. For instance, one of you can carry food-related and fire-building, while the other can carry shelter-related. Smaller packs for the kids, with clothing basics, can also carry everyone's toothbrushes. Make it fun for the kids to prepare so they won't be scared. "Hey, kids, what can we put our clothes in to keep them dry?" One-gallon ziplock bags are ideal." Rattled Awake: Volume Five

This photos of tools and instructions, make this an invaluable chapter when it comes to water purity and emergency preparation. Remember, the folks in Philadelphia had no advance warning of tainted water.

Sadly, cyber attacks on water treatment plants are occuring more often. PLEASE consider the images you will see in this chapter, and allow them to motivate you, as intended.

Return to Sender - read by Lonnee Rey

You have to go through it to get over it.
The trick is not getting stuck in it.

" ...So there I was wondering what to say to my ex stepfather father-figure jerk-off. Was what he did to me as a kid the reason behind that career? Looking over the wins, I don't know if it's something to be upset about.

"Because of that job, I was hired to be a professional radio personality on the world's first uncensored adult talk station on the web, ksexradio.com. "The Big Dick and Alexis Show" was on two hours a day, five days a week. I was the hottie with a body, and he was truly a big dick. His idea of entertainment was doing armpit farts into the microphone. Yep, he had the humor of a 10-year-old, and the intelligence to match. It took a lot of work to fill two hours a day with no commercials, no callers, no social media—nothing but a Big Dick."

"...How was any of this a bad thing? I guess it depends on how you look at it, but for me, it was part of a colorful tapestry, the life of a free spirit, learning about life in the most unusual ways. Should I be upset with him, or should I thank him? What was there to say? "Dear Maurice, in spite of you robbing me of innocence as a child, and still being a sexual predator, 'ha-ha' Pedo, my life worked-out"?

There was more damage done from his bullying and insults; invisible wounds that took decades to heal; stuff that really damages a psyche. As if he would care. That's not what this letter was for; it was to let him know I know and what he did, and how f'n uncool he still is." This chapter has a *hilarious* "Postcards for the Pissed Off" template. Check it out here: The Podcasters' Edition

Inspired by the true story, "The Man Who Saved Pinball"

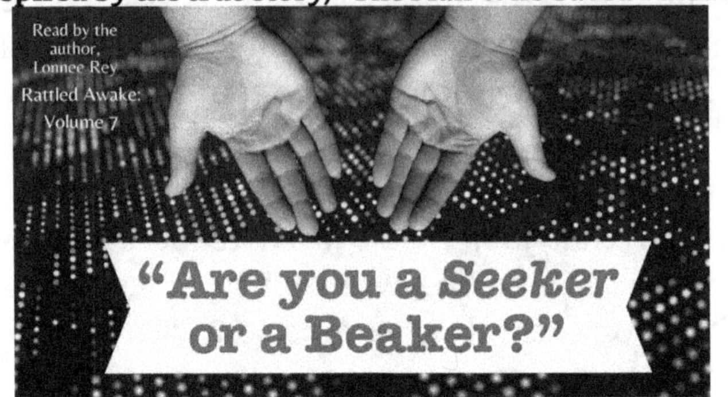

"Are you a Seeker or a Beaker?" read by author
Lonnee Rey who is Rattled Awake!!

"I am embarrassed at having been a beaker – someone who allowed others to fill my head with their La Guardia-like BS. I didn't know what I didn't know; didn't know to ask; never thought things were as messed-up as I've learned them to be. At first, cognitive dissonance, mental discomfort that results from holding two conflicting beliefs, values, or attitudes, and not being able to grasp new knowledge, shook me something fierce. The depth of betrayal at the hands of trusted sources sparked so much doubt and disbelief. Heck, I used to say, "We're all one and it's all good." It made me feel better, sure. However, it wasn't the full picture.

I was guilty of wearing rose-colored glasses caked with a lifetime residue of believing everyone was good, meant well, and wanted to help others. I paid the price for delusional thinking, too. In 2022, I published a book meant to be a field guide to spotting trouble before it becomes your problem. It was written in response to what was discovered as a Seeker: a global clown show on parade. Their behavior inspired the title, "How to Deal with a Dumbass: what to do and say when they come your way." Five red flags including "Apathy" and "Erratic" are highlighted, as are strategies to break up, break out and break free from the influence of chaos-causing people. Stories of how I blindly trusted the wrong people, a "Repeat Offender" myself, make this a humorous, memoir-esque book.

Indeed, my Polly Anna outlook got me into major hot water, over-and-over again. Becoming the poster child for what not to do also landed me featured guest roles on the Tyra Banks & Steve Harvey talk shows, so I guess that's a win -? Admitting I was blind to evil, or ill-intending people, has been embarrassing, but so what? Acknowledge, forgive and move on. Action alleviates anxiety. We are a product of our environment until we seek otherwise…" Rattled Awake: Volume Seven - Kindle

Transforming Tragedy into Destiny -

read by the author, Lonnee Rey

"Do you ever wonder if you are being subjected to fate, karma, or destiny? I sure did - still do, actually. The hardest bit is thinking you're doomed no matter what you call it. Truth is, there appears to be fated experiences. For instance, I will never forget my natal chart reading. All I wanted was some insight into my life. In my early 30s, I'd grown tired of trying to figure out my path. The group of six readers poured over it for what felt like an eternity. They finally invited me back to the chart to discuss their findings. "We see here," the spokesman said, pointing to my chart, "you were three when your parents got divorced. Are we close?" Close?! More like spot-on. How the hell are three people's futures entwined on my chart? If that doesn't make you go 'hmmm' what will?" Rattled Awake: The Writers & Poets Edition

"I was a late bloomer. You might be, too. So what?? Don't let anyone tamp you down, Honey. It could very well be that all this time has passed to ready and steady you for what is next.

The Time is Now - read by the author

The Law of Courage states:

"Fear departs where action is present."

Start here: Just allow optimism to enter. Begin asking for help from the 'write' sources, the voices of experience. It pays off if you follow-up. Listen to your "BIG Yes!" Be curious. Explore. When will it be your turn? It might just be NOW.

Remember, what calls to you is meant for you.

Everything you want is on the other side of something you haven't tried, yet."

Preconceived notions are the locks on
the door to wisdom. Mary Browne

The Liberty Issue has meaning if you choose to embody the messages you have read, and heard, with all your might.

Think global, act local.

Exercise your freedom of expression. Be a stand-up guy in your family, then in your local area, and *know* the world will be a better place because you took action.

Lonnee Rey is a 'professional tumbleweed' who has lived to tell about it, literally. Embracing "variety is the spice of life" and embodying her childhood hero, "Pippi Longstocking," her life has been an adventure into unknown territories. Reinventing herself from the inside-out, she has returned with a lantern, and a laugh, to shine the light on the path for others who want to rewrite their next chapter.

She has helped dozens of authors create books they are proud of, and is especially proud to have been editor of the Indie Book of the Year, 2023. Her books, "Life lessons learned from a lousy mother" and "How to Deal with a Dumbass: what to do and say when come your way," along with her 9th podcast, "How to Deal with a Dumbass (a spiritual perspective)," have helped others feel lighter, laugh more and live out loud.

Her transformational writing workshops turn Nervous Nellies into confident writers, speakers and podcast guests. A 14x International Best-selling writer and ghostwriter, Lonnee is always on the lookout for people who want to join the movement that is "Rattled Awake."

AN OPEN INVITATION

Reflections From Nancy O'neill

Rattled Awake: Volume 8

How my life has changed since I became a
best selling co-author in the series.

"I want to encourage anyone and everyone to share their life story. Whether it be in small chunks or a full version. You matter, and your story matters. When I tell anyone that I am co-author of an international best-selling book, I see their eyes light up, a spark of hope. Those words hold potential for them, for others they might help, as yet unexplored. Leave a legacy for your family and friends. It's time to put pen to paper and help empower others."
— Nancy O'Neill AKA 'Is this Justice' 2024.

The International Best-selling Anthology series, "Rattled Awake" is being called a movement. Over 60 writers have shared their "Better, not bitter" stories with the world. This ongoing series is dedicated to promoting messages from everyday people with an extraordinary message.

Weekend writing workshops continue to inspire both first-time writers as well as experienced writers - all of whom benefit from the collaboration as well as the training.

If you have ever wanted live coaching and help getting your thoughts down on paper, then out into the world, (in a matter of days), *this is your chance.*

"Don't Die With The Music Still In You."

-Dr. Wayne Dyer

Visit OfficialRattledAwake.com for more information about the next workshop.